CHRIST LOVED THE CHURCH

William MacDonald

Original text material by William MacDonald
Developed as a correspondence course by
Emmaus Correspondence School,
which is an extension ministry of
Emmaus Bible College
founded in 1941.

ISBN   0-940293-07-2

10111213/432109

Instructions to Students

When men think of the Church they tend to envision the vast organized system of religion which began to develop a century after the apostolic era, which became under Constantine the state religion of the Roman Empire and which today is represented by various organized religious bodies throughout the world—the Roman Catholic, the Greek Orthodox, the State Churches, the incorporated non-conformist groups. But is that what is meant by "the Church" in the New Testament? What is God's view of the Church? What was it originally like? What should it be like today?

This course is an attempt to let the Bible speak on the subject. To some the thoughts expressed will be new, even revolutionary. Others will recognize a pattern with which they have long been familiar. All will be challenged when faced again and again with an authoritative "Thus saith the Lord." May this study be a blessing to you.

LESSONS YOU WILL STUDY

HOW TO STUDY

Begin by asking God to open your heart to receive the truths He would teach you from His Word. Read the lesson through at least twice, once to get the general drift of its contents and then again, slowly, looking up all Scripture references and examining all footnotes.

EXAMS

Each exam covers two lessons. (Exam 1, for example, covers lessons 1 and 2.) Each exam is clearly marked to show you which questions deal with which lesson. You may take the exam in two stages. When you have completed lesson 1, you may take the part of Exam 1 dealing with that lesson.

You may use any version of the Bible for general study. When answering exam questions, however, restrict yourself to either the *Authorized (King James) Version* (1611), *New King James Version* (1982) or the *American Standard Version* (1901). These are two widely used versions. There are so many versions today that your instructor cannot possibly check them all in evaluating your work.

1. Thought and Research Questions

Some exams contain questions designed to make you do original Bible study. You may use your Bible to answer these questions. They are clearly marked.

2. What Do You Say? Questions

Questions headed in this way are optional and no point value is assigned to them. You may freely state your own opinions in answer to such questions. Your candid answers will help your instructor get to know you better as an individual. They will also help us evaluate the general effectiveness of this course.

3. **How Your Papers are Graded**

Any incorrectly answered questions will be marked by your instructor. You will be referred back to the place in the Bible or the textbook where the correct answer is to be found.

RECORD YOUR GRADES

When you send in your first exam a Grade Record Card will be returned to you showing your grade for the lesson(s) just corrected. You must return this card to the School each time you send in further exams.

GROUP ENROLLMENTS

If you are enrolled in a class, submit your exam papers to the leader or secretary of the class who will send them for the entire group to the Correspondence School.

GENERAL INSTRUCTIONS

Begin studying immediately, or, if you are in a group, as soon as the group begins. Try to keep a regular study schedule. You will be allowed a maximum of one year to complete this course from the time of enrollment.

HOW YOUR PAPERS ARE GRADED

Any incorrectly answered questions will be marked by your instructor. You will be referred back to the place in the Bible or the textbook where the correct answer is to be found.

The Church Which Is His Body

"Christ loved the church and gave Himself for it." We, too, should love the church and, in a sense, should give ourselves for it. We should give ourselves in loving, glad service—sacrificially and devotedly—in order that the church on earth might progress and prosper and triumph.

The object of this course is to examine some of the more important principles of the New Testament governing the character and conduct of the "church which is His body." The general approach will be to review the great, unchangeable verities concerning the church universal, and then to show how each local assembly is responsible to witness to these truths in life and practice.

At the very outset, it should be emphasized that correctness of church position must never be divorced from correctness of condition, that the Christians who comprise a local church must always be themselves a living testimony to the truth. This emphasis will continue throughout these studies.

Turning now to the church universal, we will begin by defining and describing it.

DEFINITION OF THE CHURCH

In the New Testament, the word *church* is a translation of the Greek word *ekklesia,* which means "a called-out company," "a gathering" or an "assembly." Stephen used the word to describe Israel as "the church

1

(assembly) in the wilderness" (Acts 7:38). It is also used in the book of Acts to describe a heathen mob at Ephesus (Acts 19:32, 39, 41). But the most common use of the word in the New Testament is to describe a group of believers in the Lord Jesus Christ. Thus Paul speaks of "the *church* of God, which He hath purchased with His own blood" (Acts 20:28). In his first letter to the Corinthian Christians, the great apostle divides the whole world into Jews, Gentiles, and the *church* of God (1 Corinthians 10:32). Again, he identifies the *church* of God as including the group of Christian believers whom he persecuted before his conversion (1 Corinthians 15:9).

It has often been said that the church is not an organization but an organism. By this is meant that it is not a lifeless institution but a living unit. It is a fellowship of all those who share the life of Christ and who are linked together in living union by the Holy Spirit. It has been well called "a pure communion of persons without institutional character."

Many descriptive titles are given to the church in the New Testament, and one of the best ways of arriving at an understanding of the church is to consider the significance of each title. The following are the prominent descriptions of the church:

1. **A flock** (John 10:16, R.V.).

The Jewish nation was a fold. The church is a flock. In John 10:16 the Lord Jesus said, "Other sheep I have which are not of this fold (Israel): them also I must bring, and they shall hear my voice; and there shall be one flock (R.V.) and one Shepherd." The idea of a *flock* brings before our minds a group of Christians living together under the loving, tender care of the Good Shepherd—hearing His voice and following Him.

2. **God's husbandry** (1 Corinthians 3:9).

The church is God's garden plot in which He purposes to raise fruit for His glory. The thought of fruit-bearing is thus brought before us here.

2

3. **God's building** (1 Corinthians 3:9).

This expression pictures God as carrying on a building program. He is adding living stones to the church. How important it is that our lives should be devoted to the construction project in which He is so vitally interested!

4. **The temple of God** (1 Corinthians 3:16).

The word "temple" immediately brings before us the thought of worship, and reminds us that the only worship God gets today is from those who are members of the church.

5. **The body of Christ** (Ephesians 1:22, 23).

The body is the vehicle by which a person expresses himself. Thus the body of Christ is the unit through which the Lord chooses to express Himself to the world today. Once this great truth is grasped, a believer will never again think of the church as of minor importance, but will devote himself unreservedly to the best interests of the body of Christ.

6. **A new man** (Ephesians 2:15).

Here the idea of a new creation is prominent. The greatest of all differences among men—that of Jew and Gentile—has been abolished in the church, and God makes of these two peoples one new man.

7. **An habitation of God** (Ephesians 2:22).

This expression conveys the truth that God now dwells in the church, rather than in a material tabernacle or temple, as in the Old Testament.

8. **The bride of Christ** (Ephesians 5:25-27; 2 Corinthians 11:2).

This view of the church gives prominence to the idea of affection. "Husbands, love your wives, even as Christ also loved the church, and gave Himself for it; that He might sanctify and cleanse it with the washing of water by the word; that He might present it to Himself a glorious church, not having spot, or wrinkle, or any such thing, but that it should be holy and without blemish." If Christ loved the church, and gave Himself for it, then obviously the church should be filled with bridal affection for Him.

9. **The house of God** (1 Timothy 3:15).

A house (or household) speaks to us of order and discipline. The thought of order is suggested in 1 Timothy 3:15: "That thou mayest know how thou oughtest to behave thyself in the house of God." Discipline is suggested in 1 Peter 4:17: "Judgment must begin at the house of God."

10. **The pillar and ground of the truth** (1 Timothy 3:15).

In addition to being a support for a building, a pillar was often used in early days for posting public notices. It was a means of proclamation. The word "ground" means a bulwark or a support. Thus the church of God is the unit which He has ordained for proclaiming, supporting, and defending His truth. We may safely say, therefore, that if Christians are to be in the current of God's will and purposes, they should devote their finest efforts to the expansion and spiritual welfare of the church.

THE MISSION OF THE CHURCH

Many boast today that their mission is to preach the gospel, and they take a detached view of anything to do with the church. They should notice that the Apostle Paul's ministry was twofold: (1) "To preach

4

among the Gentiles the unsearchable riches of Christ," and also (2) "To make all men see what is the fellowship of the mystery," that is, to ground them in the great truths of the church (Ephesians 3:8, 9).

ORIGIN OF THE CHURCH

Great and godly men have differed widely as to the time of the beginning of the church. Many believe that the assembly is a continuation or outgrowth of Israel in the Old Testament. Others maintain stoutly that the church did not exist in the Old Testament, but that it began in the new dispensation. In favor of the latter viewpoint are three considerations.

In Ephesians 3:4, 5, Paul speaks of the church as a "mystery which in other ages was not made known unto the sons of men, as it is now revealed unto His holy apostles and prophets by the Spirit." Again in verse 9 he states that the church is a "mystery which from the beginning of the world hath been hid in God." (See also Colossians 1: 26; Romans 16:25, 26.) Thus the church was a secret, kept by God throughout the Old Testament times, and never revealed until the New Testament apostles and prophets appeared.

In Matthew 16:18, the Lord Jesus said, "Upon this rock *I will build* my church." In other words, the church was still future at the time He spoke.

Again in Ephesians 4:8-10, Paul emphasizes that it was the risen, ascended Christ who gave gifts to the church. This argues strongly that if the church existed before His ascension, it must have lacked gifts for its edification.

We believe it is not only possible to show that the church began in the new dispensation, but, more specifically, that it was brought into being on the day of Pentecost.

The body of Christ is said to have been formed by the baptism of the Holy Spirit (1 Corinthians 12:13). Can we determine then when the baptism of the Holy Spirit took place? In Acts 1:5, immediately prior to the Lord's ascension, He promised the apostles, "Ye shall be baptized with the Holy Ghost not many days hence." On the day of Pentecost,

5

"they were all filled with the Holy Ghost, and began to speak with other tongues as the Spirit gave them utterance" (Acts 2:4). By the time we reach Acts 5:11, the church has definitely come into being, because we read that "great fear came upon all the church. . . ."

This certainly seems to pin-point the birthday of the church as occurring at Pentecost.

When you have mastered this lesson, take the first part of Exam 1 (covering lesson 1), questions 1-7 on pages **13-15** (right after lesson 2).

Great Truths About the Church

Interwoven throughout the Acts and the Epistles of the New Testament are many grand truths concerning the church of God. Here we will comment briefly on seven of the more important ones, with the thought of developing them more completely later.

THERE IS ONE BODY

According to Ephesians 4:4 there is only one church. In spite of all the circumstances that seem to deny it, the fact remains that as far as God is concerned, there is only one body of believers on the earth today. Although this church is never visible to man in its entirety, yet it is formed into a common body by the Holy Spirit.

CHRIST IS THE HEAD OF THE BODY

By using the analogy of the human body (Ephesians 5:23; Colossians 1:18), Paul teaches us that Christ as Head in heaven controls His body on earth. The head speaks of authority, leadership, and the seat of the intellect. The head and the body share the same life, interests and prospects. As the head is not complete without the body, so, in a very real sense, Christ is not complete without His church. Thus we read in Ephesians 1:23 that the church, as His body, "is the *fulness of Him* that filleth all in all." This is cause for deepest awe and worship in the believer.

7

ALL BELIEVERS ARE MEMBERS OF THE BODY

The moment a person is saved, he is added to the church as a member of the body (Acts 2:47). This membership transcends the bounds of race, color, nationality, temperaments, culture, social caste, language and denomination.

In his classic passage on the members of Christ's body (1 Corinthians 12:12-26), Paul reminds us that there are many members in the body (vv. 12-14). Every member has a function to perform (vv. 15-17). However, not all members have the same function (v. 19). The welfare of the body depends on all the members working together (vv. 21-23). Because all the members of the body need each other, there is no cause for envy or discontent, on the one hand (vv. 15-17); or for pride and independence on the other (v. 21). Because all are members of the one body, there should be mutual care, sympathy, and joy (vv. 23-26).

THE HOLY SPIRIT IS THE REPRESENTATIVE
OF CHRIST IN THE CHURCH

After He ascended back into heaven, the Lord Jesus sent the Holy Spirit to be His Representative on the earth (John 14:16, 26). The Spirit's activities in the church may be seen in part from the fact that He leads Christians in their worship (Ephesians 2:18); He inspires their prayers (Romans 8:26, 27); He empowers their preaching (1 Thessalonians 1:5); He guides them in their activities, both positively (Acts 13:2), and negatively (Acts 16:6, 7); He raises up overseers for the church (Acts 20:28); He bestows gifts for its growth and effectiveness (Ephesians 4:11) and He guides believers into all truth (John 16:13).

THE CHURCH OF GOD IS HOLY

God is calling out of the nations a people for His name. He sets them apart to Himself from the sinful world and calls upon them to respond with lives of practical holiness (1 Corinthians 3:17). Only in this way can the church faithfully represent a holy God in this corrupt scene.

GIFTS ARE GIVEN FOR THE EDIFICATION OF THE CHURCH

It is the Lord's will that the church should grow both spiritually and numerically. To that end the risen Christ gives gifts to the church (Ephesians 4:11). These gifts are men who are given special ability to build up the church. As listed in Ephesians 4:11, the gifts are apostles, prophets, evangelists, pastors and teachers.[1]

We believe that the apostles and prophets were concerned primarily with the foundation of the church (Ephesians 2:20). The need for these apostles and New Testament prophets passed when the foundation was laid, and we no longer have them, in the primary sense of the terms.[2]

However, we still do have evangelists, pastors, and teachers. The evangelists go out to the world with the Gospel, bring sinners to Christ,

---

[1] In 1 Corinthians 12:8-10, another list of spiritual gifts is given: the word of wisdom, the word of knowledge, faith, the gifts of healing, the working of miracles, prophecy, discerning of spirits, divers kinds of tongues, and interpretation of tongues. There is no necessary contradiction between the two lists. In Ephesians 4, the gifts are persons whose whole career, apparently, is given over to evangelism, teaching, or pastoral work. In 1 Corinthians 12, the gifts are endowments or abilities which are not necessarily limited to certain individuals but which the Holy Spirit may give to any member of the Body of Christ at any time He chooses. For instance, any Christian man may be Spirit-led to give a "word of wisdom" or a "word of knowledge" and yet not be exactly a teacher. Another may be able to point a soul to Christ and yet not be an evangelist.

Again in 1 Corinthians 12:28, Paul speaks of apostles, prophets, teachers, miracles, gifts of healing, helps, governments, and diversities of tongues. The question inevitably arises here as to whether we still have gifts of a miraculous nature today. In Hebrews 2:4, it is stated that God used signs and wonders to authenticate the early preaching of the Gospel. This was in days before the complete Word of God was available in written form. Many believe that with the coming of the complete Bible, the need for these miracles ceased. The Bible does not settle the matter decisively. While we believe that these miracle gifts are not with us today, generally speaking, yet we cannot say that the sovereign Spirit is not at liberty to use them still, especially on those mission fields where the Scriptures are not extensively available. In any event, those who do profess to have these miraculous gifts must be careful to use them in accordance with the instructions of the Word (for example, the use of tongues is regulated in 1 Corinthians 14).

[2] In a secondary sense, we doubtless still have apostles, if we simply mean men sent forth by the Lord. In this lesser sense, we still have prophets also, that is, men who cry out for God against sin and abuse. But we utterly reject the idea that there are men today who have the same authority as was committed to the original apostles or who can speak by the same direct and inspired revelation as the New Testament prophets.

9

and then lead them into the fellowship of the local church. Pastors take a shepherd-care of the flock, nourishing the sheep, encouraging them, and guarding them from evil. The teachers unfold the Word of God in an understandable way, and present the doctrines of the Scriptures in a well-balanced manner.

As these gifts minister, the church grows and the saints are built up in their most holy faith. Gifts are God's provision for the expansion of the church.

ALL BELIEVERS ARE PRIESTS OF GOD

A final truth which we will mention in connection with the church is the priesthood of all believers (1 Peter 2:5, 9). In the Old Testament, only a certain group of men were eligible for the priesthood—the tribe of Levi and the family of Aaron (Exodus 28:1). Today there is no special caste of men, separate from their fellows, with distinctive garb and peculiar privileges. All children of God are priests of God with all the privileges and responsibilities that go with such a name.

THE COMPLETION AND DESTINY OF THE CHURCH

As has already been noted, the church is now in the process of construction. Every time a soul is saved, a living stone is added to the building. The edifice is rising silently without sound of hammer. The Holy Spirit adds daily to the church such as should be saved (Acts 2: 47).

One day soon, the work will be finished. The last stone will be added, and the Lord Jesus will descend into the air. As if drawn by a divine magnet, the church will rise to meet the Savior, and together they both will return to the many mansions of the Father's house. And so shall we ever be with the Lord" (1 Thessalonians 4:17).

It will be the church's blessed portion not only to be with Christ forever, but also to share the glories which He won during His earthly career (John 17:22).

Throughout eternity the church is destined to be an eternal witness to the glory of God. "That in the ages to come He might show the exceeding riches of His grace in His kindness toward us through Christ Jesus" (Ephesians 2:7).

In the meantime, the church is God's masterpiece on the earth—an object lesson to principalities and powers in heavenly places of the manifold wisdom of God. Every believer should therefore be vitally interested in the church, and his Christian service should have the expansion and edification of the church as one of its primary aims.

When you are ready, complete Exam 1 by answering questions 8-16 on pages 15-18. (You should have already answered questions 1-7 as part of your study of lesson 1.)

CHRIST LOVED THE CHURCH

Exam
Name_____ Grade_____
(print plainly)

Address _____

Zip   Class
City_____ State _____ Code _____ Number _____

Instructor _____

LESSON 1

In the blank space in the right-hand margin write the letter of the correct answer.
(20 points)

1. The title of this course is taken from
a. Acts 2:41
b. Matthew 18:15-17
c. Ephesians 5:25
d. Galatians 2:20   _____

2. The word "ekklesia"
a. is the word most commonly used in the Hebrew Old Testament to describe the church
b. is used exclusively in the New Testament in reference to the church
c. is used in the New Testament to define the local church but not the church universal
d. primarily refers to an assembly or a called-out company _____

3. The church may best be described as
a. the kingdom of God
b. a living organism
c. God's vineyard
d. the heavenly tabernacle   _____

13

4. The Lord Jesus spoke of the church
   a. on many occasions, always with an appropriate Scripture from the Old Testament
   b. as being something yet future when He was on earth
   c. as being dependent for its edification upon the gifts He would bestow upon it after His ascension
   d. as being the major subject of Old Testament revelation _____

5. Match the following list of descriptive titles for the church with the proper Scripture reference taken from the list supplied below. Just write the identifying number (1, 2, etc.) on the appropriate line. *(10 points)*

   (1) John 10:16   (5) 1 Timothy 3:15
   (2) 1 Corinthians 3:9   (6) 1 Corinthians 3:16
   (3) Ephesians 5:25-27   (7) Ephesians 1:22, 23
   (4) Ephesians 2:15

   a. The body of Christ _____

   b. The house of God _____

   c. The bride of Christ _____

   d. A flock _____

   e. God's building _____

6. You strike up a conversation with the person next to you on a plane. You find out he's a Christian. He says he is a "free-lance evangelist" and explains that soul-winning is what counts with him. He says he has little or no contact with the church. Based on what you have learned in this lesson, how would you show him he should consider the church important. Give an appropriate Scripture reference. *(10 points)*

   _____

   _____

   _____

   _____

   _____

7. List in order the four steps given in the lesson which would pin-point the church's birthday as being the day of Pentecost. *(10 points)*

a. _____ _____

_____

b. _____

_____

c. _____

_____

d. _____

_____

LESSON 2

In the blank space in the right-hand margin write the letter of the correct answer. (30 points)

8. Ephesians 4:4
a. gives scriptural warrant for denominationalism
b. emphasizes the truth that there is really only one church
c. foretold the division of the church into many factions
d. likens the denominations to the various regiments of an army _____

9. To say that Christ is not complete without the church is
a. warranted by Scripture
b. so self-evident a truth that Scripture refrains from mentioning it
c. to attack the deity and essential Godhead of Jesus
d. to make a completely unscriptural statement _____

10. A person becomes a member of the body of Christ
a. the moment he is saved
b. when he is baptized in water
c. at the time of his first communion service
d. when he is formally received onto the roll of a local church _____

11. Because all Christians belong to the one body, it follows that
   a. all Christians need each other
   b. Christians function within the church in various ways
   c. pride and a spirit of independence are contrary to common sense
   d. all the above are true _____

12. According to Acts 20:28, the Holy Spirit
   a. leads Christians in their worship
   b. bestows on the church gifts for its growth and effectiveness
   c. raises up overseers for the church
   d. empowers Christians to preach _____

13. Of the lists of gifts given in the New Testament and mentioned in this lesson, one refers to persons and not to spiritual abilities. The list is:
   a. 1 Corinthians 12:8-10
   b. Ephesians 4:11-12
   c. 1 Corinthians 12:28
   d. Romans 12:6-8 _____

14. The church will
   a. continue in its present form until the end of time
   b. wax and wane in its influence until finally it enters a decline from which it will never recover
   c. ultimately convert the whole world at which time it will be complete
   d. be taken miraculously from the earth to meet the Lord in the air _____

15. Describe the functions of each of the following. *(10 points)*

   a. The Evangelist.

   _____

   _____

   _____

   _____

16

b. The Pastor.

_____

_____

_____

_____

c. The Teacher.

_____

_____

_____

_____

16. Discuss briefly the question as to whether we still have gifts of a miraculous nature today. *(10 points)*

_____

_____

_____

_____

_____

_____

_____

_____

WHAT DO YOU SAY?

Are you a member of the New Testament Church? Describe how you became a member.

_____

_____

_____

_____

_____

The Local Church

WHAT IS IT?

In the previous pages we have discussed the church universal, which has also been called the church invisible and the mystical body of Christ.

In addition to this, the New Testament also speaks of local churches composed of believers in any given locality. Thus, we read of the churches or assemblies at Jerusalem, Corinth, Rome, and so forth. These were the local expressions of the church of God. Each one was a sovereign unit, independent of other churches, though there was fellowship between them, and all were subject to Christ.

1. The Local Church Defined

Down through the years, there has been considerable disagreement as to what constitutes a New Testament church. The usual approach is to list a certain number of requirements or marks; if a group of Christians answers to these qualifications, then it is considered to be a true local church.

Henry Barrow has given what might be considered a rather typical definition of a church. He defined it as follows: "A true-planted and rightly-established church of Christ is a company of faithful people, separated from unbelievers, gathered in the Name of Christ, whom they truly worship and readily obey. They are a brotherhood, a communion of saints, each one of them standing in and for their Christian liberty to practice whatsoever God has commanded and revealed unto them in His Holy Word."

Other definitions have been far more restricted with the result that only the churches of a certain denomination or group actually qualify.

2. The New Testament Approach

This raises a very real question. Does the New Testament list a certain number of requisites or essentials of a local church? Are the marks of an assembly stated so clearly that any believer could separate the fellowships in any area into those which are true New Testament churches and those which are not?

We would suggest that this is not the case. If becoming a true church were merely a matter of conforming to a certain pattern or going through a specified routine of meetings, then this could be done quite mechanically without spiritual exercise. Lethargy and complacency would result. Though the position of a church might be ever so correct, yet the condition of the believers might be far otherwise.

Instead of that, we believe that the New Testament approach is this. All believers are instructed that, by the grace of God, they are members of the church. They are exhorted to gather together in such a way as to give expression to the great truths of the church. Some assemblies of Christians give a very poor representation of the body of Christ. Other groups present a more faithful likeness. None does so perfectly.

Thus, instead of following the legalistic method which says, "If you meet certain requirements, you will become a church," the language of Scripture is the language of grace; namely, "You as believers are the church; now meet in such a manner as to give an accurate expression of this fact to the world." The motive power under grace is love for the Savior, and this love should make us want to present a faithful image of the body of Christ to those around us.

3. A Brief Summary

To summarize then, the local church should be a miniature of the church universal. It should *be* nothing and *do* nothing that would contradict the great truths of the church which is the body of Christ.

As Ridout has said: "Its nature and unity must be manifested. It must be seen that it is the body of Christ, formed by and indwelt by the Holy Spirit, that all believers are members of it, united to Christ glorified and to one another; that the Lord's coming is the hope before it; and that the Name of Christ is the only one by which it is called. Furthermore, it must exhibit the unity of the body of Christ."[1]

If then the local church must be a replica of the complete church, what are the great truths of the body of Christ to which it must provide a living testimony? We have already referred to seven of these fundamental truths; namely:

A. There is one body.
B. Christ is Head of the body.
C. All believers are members of the body.
D. The Holy Spirit is the Vicar of Christ in the church.
E. The church of God is holy.
F. Gifts are given for the edification of the church.
G. All believers are priests of God.

Our present objective, therefore, is to take these truths one by one, and seek to determine how the local assembly can portray them to the world.

THE TRUTH OF THE ONE BODY

The first truth to which the local church is responsible to witness is that there is one body. How can believers testify to this fact today?

---

[1]Ridout, Samuel, *The Church According to Scripture* (New York: Loizeaux Bros., Inc., 1926), p. 23.

1.   What Name Should Be Taken

Perhaps the most obvious way is by adopting no names that would separate them from other Christians. In the church of Corinth, some were saying, "I am of Paul," "I am of Apollos," or "I am of Christ." Paul indignantly condemns such a spirit by asking, "Is Christ divided?" (1 Corinthians 1:10-17).

Today Christians divide themselves into denominations named after countries, religious leaders, ordinances, or forms of church government. All such are a practical denial of the unity of the body of Christ.

Clearly, the scriptural approach is for God's children to be known only by such names as are given in the Bible—names such as "believers" (Acts 5:14); "disciples" (Acts 9:1); "Christians" (Acts 11:26); "saints" (Ephesians 1:1); and "brethren" (James 2: 1). It is perhaps one of the most difficult tasks in the Christian life to carry no name but that of a simple believer. The vast majority today feels that one must belong to some organized church and carry some other name than those given in the Word. Anyone who refuses to be known as anything but a child of God will suffer reproach at the hands even of other Christians and will always be a conundrum in the community. Yet how can believers consistently do otherwise?

But obviously it is not enough just to have a scripturally accurate name. It is all too possible to adhere strictly to the language of the Bible and yet be extremely sectarian in spirit. Some in Corinth were saying, "I am of Christ," for instance. Perhaps they prided themselves òn the correctness of their name, but they actually meant that they were of Christ to the exclusion of other true believers. Paul found fault with them equally as much as with those who claimed loyalty to himself or Apollos.

2.   What About the Denominations?

When any doubt is voiced as to the scripturalness of denominations, the objection is commonly raised that the Lord has richly

22

blessed in some of the great divisions and sects of the church. Granting that this is true, we should still remember that the blessing of the Lord does not indicate divine approval in every detail. He honors His own Word though often its delivery is accompanied by much failure and imperfection. If God blessed only where there was perfection, there would be no blessing. Therefore the fact that any group has seen His hand does not mean that He approves of all that the group does. The message is always greater than the messenger.

The Lord's attitude toward divisions in the church is clearly shown in 1 Corinthians 3:4: "For while one saith, I am of Paul; and another, I am of Apollos; are ye not carnal?"

Divisions in the church bring great evils. They create artificial barriers to fellowship. They limit the movement of gifted men of God whose ministry should be available to all the church. They confuse the world, causing men to ask, "Which church is right?"

In his renowned work, *The Lord's Prayer for Believers*, Marcus Rainsford wrote: "For my own part, I believe sects and denominations to be the result of the devil's attempt to mar and hinder as far as possible the visible union of the church of God; and that they all have their root in our spiritual pride and selfishness, our self-sufficiency and our sin.[1]

"May God forgive us for, and correct our divisions! Nothing gives greater occasion to the outside world, than the differences between professing Christians. The bickerings and contentions between men and women of different sects and denominations of the visible church of God has always been one of the world's greatest hindrances. Instead of looking on, and being constrained to confess, 'See how these Christians love one another,' the world has too often reason to say, 'See how they carp at one another, see how they judge one another, see how they malign one another.' "[2]

---

[1] Rainsford, Marcus, *The Lord's Prayer for Believers* (London: Chas. J. Thynne, 1903), p. 409.
[2] Ibid., p. 446.

3. True Unity

Believers who determine to witness to the unity of the body of Christ will find it a great difficulty to separate themselves from all divisions in the church, and at the same time maintain a loving spirit toward all the people of God.

C. H. Mackintosh, beloved author of the *Notes on the Pentateuch,* wrote: "The grand difficulty is to combine a spirit of intense separation with a spirit of grace, gentleness and forbearance; or, as another has said, 'to maintain a narrow circle with a wide heart.' This is really a difficulty. As the strict and uncompromising maintenance of truth tends to narrow the circle around us, we all shall need the expansive power of grace to keep the heart wide and the affections warm. If we contend for truth otherwise than in grace, we shall only yield a one-sided and most unattractive testimony. And on the other hand, if we try to exhibit grace at the expense of truth, it will prove, in the end, to be only the manifestation of a popular liberty at God's expense— a most worthless thing."[1]

W. H. Griffith Thomas expressed the same thought in his book, *Ministerial Life and Work:* "Let the principles be firmly fixed on the unmistakable rock of Divine truth, but let the sympathies go out as widely as possible to all who are endeavoring to live and labor for Christ. Never shall I forget the words of the saintly and noble Bishop Whipple of Minnesota, the Apostle of the Indians, as I heard them in London on a memorable occasion: 'For thirty years I have tried to see the face of Christ in those who have differed from me.' "[2]

The visible display of the unity of the body of Christ is not to be brought about by the various ecumenical movements about which so much is heard today. Such unions, councils or federations succeed only by compromising the great truths of the

---

[1] Mackintosh, C. H., "The Unequal Yoke" in *Miscellaneous Notes* (New York: Loizeaux Bros., Inc.), Vol. II, p. 29.

[2] Thomas, W. H. Griffith, *Ministerial Life and Work* (Chicago: Moody Colportage, 1927), pp. 115, 116.

Scripture. Christian congregations deny their Lord when they join with those who repudiate the virgin birth of Christ, His sinless humanity, His substitutionary death, His bodily resurrection, His ascension and exaltation, and His coming again.

The true basis of Christian unity is a common devotion to Christ and His Word. When His glory is the great desire of our hearts, then we will be drawn together, and then His prayer will be answered: "That they may be one, even as we are one" (John 17:22). As Griffith Thomas has said, "It has often been pointed out that when the tide is out, there are little pools of water here and there on the shore, separated from each other by vast stretches of sand, and it is only when the great tide rolls in and submerges them all in its vast embrace that they become one and are united. So must it be, so will it be with our severances of heart, 'our unhappy divisions'; the great tide of God's love will flow deeper and fuller into each and all of our lives, and in the ocean of that love we realize the Divine ideal of love, joy, peace for evermore."[1]

In the meantime the responsibility of local churches is to seek to maintain a testimony to the unity of the body of Christ in a day when most of Christendom serves only to deny the fact. They can do this by acknowledging in spirit, principle and practice all their fellow-believers.

---

[1] W. H. Griffith Thomas, op. cit., p. 116.

When you have mastered this lesson, take the first part of Exam 2 (covering lesson 3), questions 1-10 on pages **33-35** (right after lesson 4).

The Headship of Christ

CHRIST THE HEAD

A second truth to which the local church should be a witness is that Christ is the Head of the body. How can believers testify to this fact today? Obviously they must accept no human leader as head of the church. The most glaring violation of this is the head of a large religious system who claims to be the temporal head of the body of Christ. Most Christians today have seen the folly of such a pretension, yet in somewhat subtler forms the evil has infiltrated into almost all segments of Christendom.

The headship of Christ is truly acknowledged when He is allowed to control the church's activities, to make its decisions, to superintend in every department. To many this will sound vague and impractical. How can the Lord in heaven guide a local church on earth? The answer is that He will never fail to make His will known to those who patiently wait on Him for it. True, this requires a great deal of spiritual exercise on the part of the believers. It would be much easier to take matters in their own hands, and make their own plans. But it should be remembered that New Testament principles can only be carried out with New Testament power, and those who are unwilling to tread the path of dependence, prayer, and patient waiting will never have the privilege of seeing the Great Head of the church guiding the local assembly here on earth.

At this point it might be appropriate to emphasize that it is one thing to give lip-service to the Headship of Christ and quite another thing to acknowledge it practically. There are some who apparently would shed their blood for the truth of the Headship of Christ, and yet who deny it practically by being virtual dictators in the assembly. A man or a group of men may not have any official title or designation in a church and yet rule it ruthlessly. Diotrephes was such a man (3 John 9, 10). He loved to have the preeminence; he prated against godly men like John with malicious words; he would not receive such men, and forbade those who would, casting them out of the church. This was a positive denial of Christ as Head.

Perhaps a word should be added concerning the headquarters of the church. The word *headquarters* speaks of the center of operations and of authority. The headquarters of the church are where the Head is; namely, in heaven. A local church cannot consistently recognize any controlling organization such as a synod, presbytery, or council where control is exercised over a single church or a group of churches. Each assembly stands directly responsible to the Head of the church, and should be nothing and do nothing that would deny that truth.

RECEPTION POLICY

As pointed out previously, a third important truth in connection with the church is that all believers are members of the body. It is the duty of the assembly to set forth this truth with accuracy and faithfulness. Nothing that it teaches or practices should deny the oneness of all Christians. If we inquire how the local church can witness to this, we shall find ourselves concerned with the policies it follows in receiving others into its fellowship. This subject is commonly known as reception policy, and the principles are clear.

1. The General Rule

The general principle is that the assembly should receive all those whom Christ has received. "Wherefore receive ye one another as Christ also received us to the glory of God" (Romans 15:7). The basis of true fellowship is the fact that a person has already been received into the body of Christ. The local church merely gives visible expression to that fact by welcoming him into its midst.

2.   Exceptions to the Rule

However, this is not a rule without exception. There are three additional requirements which are implicit in the teachings of the New Testament. The person received must be holy in life (1 Corinthians 5:11; 10:21). It would obviously give a very inaccurate representation of the holy character of the church to receive a fornicator, a covetous man, an idolater, a railer, a drunkard or an extortioner.

Closely associated with this is the fact it would be quite improper to receive a person who was at the time under discipline by another local church (1 Corinthians 5:13). This would be a denial of the unity of the body of Christ (Ephesians 4:4). Until an excommunicated person has been restored to fellowship with the Lord and with His people, he is counted as a heathen man and a publican (Matthew 18:17).

Finally, the person must be sound as to the doctrine of Christ (2 John 10). "If there come any unto you and bring not this doctrine, receive him not into your house, neither bid him God speed." The question arises here as to what is included in the doctrine of Christ. The expression is not explained in this passage, but we would suggest that the doctrine of Christ includes the great truths concerning His Person and Work: namely, His deity, His virgin birth, His sinless life, His substitutionary death, His burial, resurrection and ascension, and His coming again.

To summarize then, we would conclude that a local church should receive into its fellowship all born-again believers who are holy in life, not under discipline by some other assembly, and sound in doctrine.

3.   Other Pertinent Rules

But the Scriptures give us some other instructions as to the matter of reception. The local assembly should:

a. Receive him who is weak in the faith (Romans 14:1). This refers to a Christian who is unduly scrupulous with regard to matters of moral indifference. The fact that he is a vegetarian, for instance, should not exclude him.

b. Receive without respect of persons (James 2:1-5). The Bible warns against showing special consideration to the rich, and despising the poor. This would apply too in the matter of race, social level, or culture. Discrimination is unchristian.

c. Receive on the basis of life, not light (Acts 9:26-38). Fellowship is not dependent on how much one knows, but rather on the Person whom he knows. Thus, Apollos was received in Ephesus, even though his knowledge was quite defective (Acts 18:24-28).

d. Receive on the basis of life, not of ordinance. Baptism is nowhere said to be the door to the assembly. Though it is true that all believers should be baptized (Matthew 28:19), yet the moment we say that a person *must* be baptized in order to be received into fellowship, we have gone beyond the Word.

e. Receive on the basis of life, not service. Just because we might not agree with a Christian's sphere of service is no reason for denying him the fellowship of the local church. In Luke 9:53, we read that the Samaritans would not receive the Lord Jesus because His face was as though He would go to Jerusalem. They were motivated by sectarianism rather than by divine principles.

f. Receive a person in spite of what he may have been before he was saved. Paul had been a persecutor, but he was received without regard to his past history (Acts 9:27, 28). Onesimus had been a thief, but Paul exhorts Philemon to receive him (Philemon 12, 15, 17). When an assembly's doors are closed to converted drunkards, gamblers, or outcasts, it has lost its true character, and has become a social club.

g. Receive believers in the Lord with gladness (Philippians 2:29). In a very real sense, the way we treat the weakest member of His body, is the way we treat the Lord Himself. "Inasmuch as ye have done it unto one of the least of these my brethren, ye have done it unto me" (Matthew 25:40).

4. How to Know If A Person Is Saved

Now the question invariably arises, "How is an assembly to know whether a person is really saved and eligible for fellowship?" At least five possible approaches may be suggested. First, there is the use of letters of recommendation (Romans 16:1). A Christian travelling from one assembly to another can avoid considerable difficulty and embarrassment by carrying a letter from his home assembly, testifying to his faith and walk.

Then the testimony of two or three witnesses is acceptable (Matthew 18:16). If a person is known to two or more Christians in a local church, that church may receive him on their recommendation.

The testimony of only one person, but one who has the confidence of the assembly, can be taken. Paul commended Phebe to the saints at Rome (Romans 16:1), and Epaphroditus to the church at Philippi (Philippians 2:28-30).

A man's own reputation as a servant of Christ is sufficient (2 Corinthians 3:1-2). Paul disclaimed the necessity of a letter of commendation to the church at Corinth because he was well-known to them as an apostle of Jesus Christ.

There can be a careful inquiry and investigation by the assembly itself. By this is meant that an assembly, perhaps through the elders, may question a person as to his faith in Christ, etc., asking him to give a reason of the hope that is in him (1 Peter 3:15). They may then receive him after reasonable assurance that he belongs to Christ.

5. Common Problems

Before closing this section on reception, we should also consider three other questions which commonly arise in connection with this subject.

Does the church have any right to judge whether a man is saved or not? The answer is that this is not only a right but a sacred obligation. Since Christians are forbidden to have fellowship

31

with unbelievers (2 Corinthians 6:14, 17), it is obvious that they are required to use every reasonable means to discern the spiritual status of those who seek a place among the people of God.

Suppose an assembly receives a man and he subsequently teaches error in the church? Then his teaching should be publicly refuted from the Word of God (1 Timothy 5:20). The New Testament church can only function in the environment of an open Bible. It should have godly elders who can expose error and defend the faith (Titus 1:9).

Suppose a local church receives a person, and he either attends irregularly thereafter, or never comes back? In the first place it should be emphasized that fellowship means sharing or holding things in common. Those in fellowship should enter into the life of the assembly, bear their load of responsibility, and share the work involved. Strictly speaking, if a person attends only one service a week, he is really not in fellowship. With regard to a person who is received but who never returns, the man himself is accountable. The assembly is responsible to present to him a faithful and spiritual representation of the church. He is thereafter obligated to be obedient to the truth.

Obviously the subject of reception is a complicated one, and we have only been able to touch on some of its more important aspects. Recognizing the incompleteness of our coverage, we move on to the next major point.

When you are ready, complete Exam 2 by answering questions 11-20 on pages 35-38. (You should have already answered questions 1-10 as part of your study of lesson 1.)

CHRIST LOVED THE CHURCH

Name_____ Exam Grade_____
(print plainly)

Address _____

City_____ State _____ Zip Code _____ Class Number _____

Instructor _____

LESSON 3

In the blank space in the right-hand margin write the letter of the correct answer. (45 points)

1. The New Testament views local churches as
a. members of various independent denominations
b. subordinate to a central, governing denominational head-quarters
c. united in a world federation but organized along democratic lines
d. local expressions of the universal church, each sovereign and independent but in fellowship one with the other   _____

2. Henry Barrow's definition of the church
a. is far too narrow since it would embrace only the churches of one denomination
b. is far too broad since it takes in purely human concepts of the church which have no warrant in Scripture
c. is based on the list of requirements for a local church found in the key New Testament passage which deals with this subject
d. raises the question as to whether the New Testament even lists categorically the marks of a local assembly   _____

3. So far as the local church is concerned, the New Testament emphasis is on
a. the spiritual condition of the individual believer
b. the importance of baptism as the entrance into the local church
c. the specified routine of meetings which occupy the corporate life of the group
d. acceptance to the Lord's Supper as the key for determining who is in fellowship   _____

4. The local church is to be
   a. only partially like the universal church
   b. an exact miniature of the universal church
   c. quite independent of the universal church
   d. conformed to certain requirements dictated by the denomination to which it belongs _____

5. Which of the following names would be the most scriptural?
   a. Baptist
   b. Methodist
   c. Presbyterian
   d. Christian
   e. any of the above _____

6. The Corinthian believers who were most correct were those who were saying
   a. "I am of Paul"
   b. "I am of Cephas"
   c. "I am of Apollos"
   d. "I am of Christ"
   e. none of them were correct _____

7. Denominationalism
   a. has been blessed of God and must therefore be regarded as scriptural
   b. must not be regarded as scriptural simply because it has been blessed of God
   c. has never been blessed of God
   d. has been blessed of God because division leads to multiplication as in the miracle of the loaves and fishes _____

8. Denominationalism
   a. is a blessing in disguise because it provides a person with the choice of a church which best suits his particular temperament
   b. enables gifted men to develop in a variety of ways for the ultimate edification of the church universal
   c. enhances the visible union of the church of God by displaying its many glories in a multitude of different facets
   d. hinders the work of God by confusing the world _____

9. Divisions in the church can be overcome best by
   a. the ecumenical movement
   b. seeking broad areas of compromise on the issues which divide
   c. greater common devotion to the Lord, His Word and His glory
   d. persuading people to leave the denominations to join "the one true church" _____

10. A truly saved believer from a local denominational church wishes to meet temporarily with believers in your fellowship even though he does not see eye to eye on some of the truths maintained in your midst. He is sound on all the great essentials of the faith and his life is a testimony to the Lord. In view of what you have learned in this lesson, should he be received into your local fellowship? Give reasons for your answer.   *(5 points)*

_____

_____

_____

_____

_____

_____

_____

LESSON 4

In the blank space in the right-hand margin write the letter of the correct answer. (35 points)

11. It would be most true to say that
   a. the head of the church resides in Rome
   b. the church has no head
   c. Christ is the head of the church
   d. the church has many heads _____

12. Diotrephes is an illustration of a man who
   a. is the head of a local church
   b. denies the headship of Christ
   c. exemplifies in his life the doctrine that Christ is the head of the church
   d. believes the apostles occupied a unique position of headship over the church   _____

13. Which of the following would be unscriptural when associated with a group of local churches?
   a. a central headquarters
   b. a united evangelistic crusade
   c. a meeting of leading brethren from each local church convened to discuss mutual problems, goals and interests
   d. all the above   _____

14. The true basis of fellowship in a local church is
   a. membership in the body of Christ
   b. baptism
   c. acceptance by the elders (or deacons)
   d. transfer of membership from another church   _____

15. A person applies for acceptance into a local church. This person's public and private life is beyond reproach. He is not under discipline from another local church. However, conversation reveals that he does not believe in the virgin birth of Christ. Which of the following Scriptures would give the authority for refusing to receive him?
   a. 1 Corinthians 5:11
   b. 1 Corinthians 5:13
   c. 2 John 10
   d. none of them   _____

16. A brother seeks to be received into the fellowship of the local church. He is a faddist on diet and believes that proteins and carbohydrates ought not to be eaten at the same meal. He should be
   a. refused fellowship because his views are erroneous
   b. refused fellowship because his dietary peculiarities might lead to division in the assembly
   c. accepted only upon his promise to keep his views to himself and at all church functions eat the same way as other Christians
   d. accepted into the fellowship without question so long as he is sound in life and on essential doctrine   _____

17. A paroled murderer applies for fellowship in the local church. He says he was saved while in prison. Enquiry substantiates this claim. He should
a. not be received because of the nature of his crime
b. not be received because it would hinder the testimony of the local church in the neighborhood were people to know about it
c. be received
d. be received only after he had been put on probation for several years _____

18. List 3 possible approaches to discovering whether or not a person asking to be received into the local fellowship is really eligible. *(5 points)*

a. _____

_____

b. _____

_____

c. _____

_____

19. Refute the statement "we must not judge a man." *(5 points)*

_____

_____

_____

_____

20. What should be done when a person in the local fellowship teaches something unscriptural? *(5 points)*

_____

_____

_____

_____

_____

WHAT DO YOU SAY?

To what extent does your local church employ scriptural practices in determining who is to be received into the fellowship?

_____

_____

_____

_____

_____

Lesson 5

The Holy Spirit in the Church

The local church should maintain, by precept and by practice, the vital truth that the Holy Spirit is the Representative of Christ in the church. At first glance, this fact may seem to overlap or conflict with the previously discussed doctrine that Christ is the Head of the church. Both statements are true, however. Christ is the Head of the church, but has delegated the Holy Spirit to be His Agent or Representative on the earth. Therefore the obligation of every local church is to give the Spirit of God His rightful place.

PRACTICAL GUIDANCE (Acts 13:1-4)

The assembly should seek His guidance in all its affairs, whether in choosing a location for its public testimony, arranging the types of meetings to be held, discerning the human instruments to be used in ministering the Word of God, disbursement of funds, or carrying on godly discipline.

THE HOLY SPIRIT IS SOVEREIGN (1 Corinthians 12:11)

The local church should ever recognize the sovereignty of the Spirit. By this we mean that He can do as He pleases, and that He will not always choose to do things in exactly the same way, though He will never act contrary to the Word. The very symbols of the Spirit used in the Scriptures—fire, oil, water, wind—speak of fluidity, of unpredictable behavior. Thus, wise Christians will be sufficiently elastic to allow Him this divine prerogative.

It was so in the early church, but soon people became uneasy with meetings that were "free and social, with the minimum of form." Thus controls were added and formalism and ritualism took over. The Holy Spirit was quenched, and the church lost its power.

QUENCHING THE SPIRIT (1 Thessalonians 5:19)

This shift from the freedom of the Spirit to human control has been described by James Denney eloquently. Though Mr. Denny writes at some length, the reader will find his article will richly repay study. Commenting on the verse, "Quench not the Spirit," he says:

"When the Holy Spirit descended on the Church at Pentecost, 'there appeared unto them tongues parting asunder, like as of fire; and it sat upon each one of them'; and their lips were opened to declare the mighty works of God. A man who has received this great gift is described as fervent, literally, boiling, with the Spirit. The new birth in those early days was a new birth; it kindled in the soul thoughts and feelings to which it had hitherto been strange; it brought with it the consciousness of new powers; a new vision of God; a new love of holiness; a new insight into the Holy Scriptures, and into the meaning of man's life; often a new power of ardent, passionate speech. In the First Epistle to the Corinthians Paul describes a primitive Christian congregation. There was not one silent among them. When they came together every one had a psalm, a revelation, a prophecy, an interpretation. The manifestation of the Spirit had been given to each one to profit withal; and on all hands the spiritual fire was ready to flame forth. Conversion to the Christian faith, the acceptance of the apostolic Gospel, was not a thing which made little difference to men: it convulsed their whole nature to its depth; they were never the same again; they were new creatures, with a new life in them, all fervour and flame.

"A state so unlike nature, in the ordinary sense of the term, was

40

sure to have its inconveniences. The Christian, even when he had received the gift of the Holy Ghost, was still a man; and as likely as not a man who had to struggle against vanity, folly, ambition, and selfishness of all kinds. His enthusiasm might even seem, in the first instance, to aggravate, instead of removing, his natural faults. It might drive him to speak—for in a primitive church anybody who pleased might speak—when it would have been better for him to be silent. It might lead him to break out in prayer or praise or exhortation, in a style which made the wise sigh. And for those reasons the wise, and such as thought themselves wise, would be apt to discourage the exercise of spiritual gifts altogether. 'Contain yourself,' they would say to the man whose heart burned within him, and who was restless till the flame could leap out; 'contain yourself; exercise a little self-control; it is unworthy of a rational being to be carried away in this fashion.'

"No doubt situations like this were common in the church at Thessalonica. They are produced inevitably by difference of age and of temperament. The old and the phlegmatic are a natural, and, doubtless, a providential, counterweight to the young and sanguine. But the wisdom which comes of experience and of temperament has its disadvantages as compared with fervour of spirit. It is cold and unenthusiastic; it cannot propagate itself; it cannot set fire to anything and spread. And because it is under this incapacity of kindling the souls of men into enthusiasm, it is forbidden to pour cold water on such enthusiasm when it breaks forth in words of fire. That is the meaning of 'Quench not the Spirit.' The commandment presupposes that the Spirit can be quenched. Cold looks, contemptuous words, silence, studied disregard, go a long way to quench it. So does unsympathetic criticism.

"Everyone knows that a fire smokes most when it is newly kindled; but the way to get rid of the smoke is not to pour cold water on the fire, but to let it burn itself clear. If you are wise enough you may even help it to burn itself clear; by rearranging the materials, or securing a better draught; but the wisest thing most people can do when the fire has got hold is to let it alone; and that is also the wise course for most when they meet with a disciple whose zeal burns like fire. Very likely the smoke hurts their eyes; but the smoke will soon pass by; and it may well be tolerated in the meantime for the sake of heat.

For this apostolic precept takes for granted that fervour of spirit, a Christian enthusiasm for what is good, is the best thing in the world. It may be untaught and inexperienced; it may have all its mistakes to make; it may be wonderfully blind to the limitations which the stern necessities of life put upon the generous hopes of man: but it is of God; it is expansive; it is contagious; it is worth more as a spiritual force than all the wisdom in the world.

"I have hinted at ways in which the Spirit is quenched; it is sad to reflect that from one point of view the history of the church is a long series of rebellions of the Spirit. 'Where the Spirit of the Lord is,' the Apostle tells us elsewhere, 'there is liberty.' But liberty in a society has its dangers; it is, to a certain extent, at war with order; and the guardians of order are not apt to be too considerate of it. Hence it came to pass that at a very early period, and in the interests of good order, the freedom of the Spirit was summarily suppressed in the church. 'The gift of ruling,' it has been said, 'like Aaron's rod, seemed to swallow up the other gifts.' The rulers of the church became a class entirely apart from its ordinary members, and all exercise of spiritual gifts for the building up of the church was confined to them. Nay, the monstrous idea was originated, and taught as a dogma, that they alone were the depositaries, or, as it is sometimes said, the custodians, of the grace and truth of the gospel; only through them could men come into contact with the Holy Ghost. In plain English, the Spirit was quenched when Christians met for worship. One great extinguisher was placed over the flame that burned in the hearts of the brethren; it was not allowed to show itself; it must not disturb, by its eruption in praise or prayer or fiery exhortation, the decency and order of divine service. . . . I say that was the condition to which Christian worship was reduced at a very early period; and it is unhappily the condition in which, for the most part, it subsists at this moment. Do you think we are gainers by it? I do not believe it. It has always come from time to time to be intolerable. The Montanists of the second century, the heretical sects of the middle ages, the Independents and Quakers of the English Commonwealth, the lay preachers of Wesleyanism, the Salvationists, the Plymouthists, and the Evangelistic associations of our own day,—all these are in various degrees the protest of the Spirit, and its right and necessary protest, against the authority which would quench it, and by quenching it impoverish the church."[1]

The assembly, then, should never fetter the Holy Spirit, either with unscriptural rules, stereotyped program, rituals, or liturgies. How grieved He must often be by rigid understandings that a meeting must end at a certain time, that a service must always follow a certain routine, that ministry at certain stages of a worship meeting is quite unacceptable! Such regulations can only lead to a loss of spiritual power.

IF THE SPIRIT HAD HIS WAY TODAY

We might well pause to ask ourselves what it would be like in our local assemblies if the Holy Spirit were really depended on to be the Divine Leader. C. H. Mackintosh gives a vivid description of such an ideal situation, and we reproduce it here:

"We have but little conception of what an assembly would be were each one distinctly led by the Holy Ghost, and gathered only to Jesus. We should not then have to complain of dull, heavy, unprofitable, trying meetings. We should have no fear of an unhallowed intrusion of mere nature and its restless doings—no making of prayer—no talking for talking's sake—no hymnbook seized to fill a gap. Each one would know his place in the Lord's immediate presence—each gifted vessel would be filled, fitted, and used by the Master's hand—each eye would be directed to Jesus—each heart occupied with Him. If a chapter were read, it would be the very voice of God. If a word were spoken, it would tell with power upon the heart. If prayer were offered, it would lead the soul into the very presence of God. If a hymn were sung, it would lift the spirit up to God, and be like sweeping the strings of the heavenly harp. We should feel ourselves in the very sanctuary of God, and enjoy a foretaste of that time when we shall worship in the courts above and go no more out."[2]

---

[1]Denny, James, "The Epistles to the Thessalonians" in *The Expositor's Bible* (London: Hodder and Stoughton, 1902), pp. 233-238.
[2]Mackintosh, C. H., "The Assembly of God" in *Miscellaneous Writings* (New York: Loizeaux Bros., No date given), Vol. III, p. 36.

When you have mastered this lesson, take the first part of Exam 3 (covering lesson 5), questions 1-10 on pages 51-53 (right after lesson 6).

Discipline in the Church

If a local assembly is to be an accurate replica of the church of God, it must witness to a fifth vital truth. It must be holy. But how can it exhibit this in a practical way?

PREVENTION IS BETTER THAN CURE

First of all, it can do so by the godly lives of those who are associated with it. This is fundamental. God desires practical sanctification (1 Thessalonians 4:3). This is why church truths are not given as an isolated and distinct outline in any one section of the New Testament. Rather, they are found in many different places, and are interspersed with practical instruction for holy Christian living. The Lord does not simply want people who are outwardly correct in their church life, but those whose lives are testimonies to the truth.

To that end the local church should provide a good diet of Bible teaching. This instruction should not consist of mere snatches from here and there, but of consecutive, systematic teaching of the Word of God. Only in this way will the saints receive *all* the Word, and *in the balance* in which God has given it.

Though sound and systematic teaching will have a definite preventative effect as far as sin in an assembly is concerned, yet inevitably every local church will be called upon to take disciplinary action. Whenever sin comes in to affect the peace of the assembly or its testimony in the community, action must be taken. "Judgment must begin at the house of God" (1 Peter 4:17).

REASONS FOR ACTING

Disciplinary action has two principal purposes: (1) To expose and expel from the fellowship professing Christians who are actually unregenerate —such people as are described in 1 John 2:19, (2) To punish an erring believer in such a way as to bring about his restoration to the Lord and to the local church. Discipline of Christians is never an end in itself but always a means of effecting spiritual recovery.

DEGREES OF DISCIPLINE

Various degrees of discipline are described in the New Testament. In the case of a brother who sins against another, such a one should first be dealt with privately. If he will not listen, then one or two more persons should go to him. Failure to listen to this collective witness results in his being brought before the church. If this latter action should fail, then he is to be counted as an heathen man and a publican (Matthew 18:15-17).

Another form of discipline is a *warning* (1 Thessalonians 5:14). This is to be employed in the case of a brother who is unruly; that is, one who refuses to submit to those who are over him in the Lord.

Then we read that two classes of people are to be avoided: namely, a disorderly man (2 Thessalonians 3:11, 14, 15), and one who causes divisions (Romans 16:17). The disorderly person is one who refuses to work, while the other creates divisions among God's people in order to attract a following and profit materially.

An heretic should be *rejected* after the first and second warning (Titus 3:10). (There is some question as to whether this is a less severe form of discipline, or whether it amounts to excommunication.)

Then there is the extreme form of discipline—excommunication from the church (1 Corinthians 5:11, 13). This is reserved for a fornicator, a covetous man, an idolater, a railer, a drunkard or an extortioner.

THE IMPORTANCE OF PROPER EVIDENCE

An important consideration in the matter of discipline is to make sure that a case is tried fairly on the basis of reliable evidence. The general principles that apply in this regard are clearly set forth in the following summary.

"We should never allow ourselves to form, much less to express and act upon, a judgment without the testimony of two or three witnesses. However trustworthy and morally reliable any one witness may be, it is not a sufficient basis for a conclusion. We may feel convicted in our minds that the thing is true because affirmed by one in whom we have confidence; but God is wiser than we. It may be that the one witness is thoroughly upright and truthful, that he would not for worlds tell an untruth or bear false witness against any one, all this may be true, but we must adhere to the divine rule 'In the mouth of two or three witnesses shall every word be established.'

"Would that this were more diligently attended to in the church of God! Its value in all cases of discipline, and in all cases affecting the character or reputation of any one, is simply incalculable. Ere ever an assembly reaches a conclusion or acts on a judgment in any given case, it should insist on adequate evidence. If this be not forthcoming, let all wait on God—wait patiently and confidingly and He will surely supply what is needed.

"For instance, if there be moral evil or doctrinal error in an assembly of Christians, but it is only known to one; that one is perfectly certain—deeply and thoroughly convinced of the fact. What is to be done? Wait on God for further witness. To act without this is to infringe a divine principle laid down with all possible clearness again and again in the Word of God. Is the one witness to feel himself aggrieved or insulted because his testimony is not acted upon? Assuredly not; indeed he ought not to expect such a thing, yea, he ought not to come forward as a witness until he can corroborate his testimony by the evidence of

47

one or more. Is the assembly to be deemed indifferent or supine because it refuses to act on the testimony of a solitary witness? Nay, it would be flying in the face of a divine command were it to do so.

"And be it remembered that this great practical principle is not confined in its application to cases of discipline or questions connected with an assembly of the Lord's people; it is of universal application. We should never allow ourselves to form a judgment or come to a conclusion without the divinely appointed measure of evidence; if that be not forthcoming, and if it be needful for us to judge in the case, God will, in due time, furnish the needed evidence. We have known a case in which a man was falsely accused because the accuser based his charge upon the evidence of one of his senses; had he taken the trouble of getting the evidence of one or two more of his senses, he would not have made the charge."[1]

HOW TO ADMINISTER DISCIPLINE

Another aspect of this subject that deserves careful consideration is the manner in which the discipline is carried out. For example, it should be accomplished in the spirit of meekness, considering one's self, lest he also be tempted (Galatians 6:1). Also, it should be strictly impartial. The fact that a wrongdoer is related to us by ties of nature, for instance, should in no wise influence our decision in the matter. Respect of persons must not be shown (Deuteronomy 1:17; James 2:1).

In the case of excommunication, it should be the action of the assembly, and not of any one person (2 Corinthians 2:6). We refer once again to C. H. Mackintosh for the spirit in which this form of discipline should be effected. He says: "Nothing can be more solemn or affecting than the act of putting away a person from the Lord's table. It is the last sad and unavoidable act of the whole assembly, and it should be performed with broken hearts and weeping eyes. Alas how often it is otherwise! How often does this most solemn and holy duty take the

---

[1]Mackintosh, C. H., *Notes on Deuteronomy* (New York: Loizeaux Bros., Inc., No date given), Vol. II, pp. 263-265.

form of a mere official announcement that such a person is out of fellowship. Need we wonder that discipline, so carried out, fails to tell with power upon the erring one, or upon the assembly.

"How then should the discipline be carried out? Just as 1 Corinthians 5 directs. When the case is so patent, so clear, that all discussion and all deliberation is at an end, the whole assembly should be solemnly convened for the special purpose—for, most assuredly, it is of sufficient gravity and importance to command a special meeting. All should, if possible, attend, and seek grace to make the sin their own, to go down before God in true self-judgment, and eat the sin-offering. The assembly is not called to deliberate or discuss. The case should be thoroughly investigated, and all the facts collected by those who care for the interests of Christ and His church; and when it is thoroughly settled, and the evidence perfectly conclusive, then the whole assembly is called to perform, in deep sorrow and humiliation, the sad act of putting away from among themselves the evil doer. It is an act of holy obedience to the Lord's command."[1]

Finally it should not need emphasis that Christians should not broadcast the sin of their fellows, but rather throw a kindly cloke of secrecy around the sin and its discipline, as far as outsiders are concerned.

CONCLUSION

Only as the assembly takes resolute action when sin is discovered can it hope to maintain its true character as a miniature of the holy temple of God.

Perhaps it should be added here that the New Testament assumes every believer to be attached to some local church; otherwise he would be free from the discipline of any assembly, and such a freedom would be fraught with the gravest perils for the individual.

---

[1]Mackintosh, C. H., "The Discipline of the Assembly" in *Miscellaneous Writings* (New York: Loizeaux Bros., No date given), Vol. V, pp. 31, 32.

When you are ready, complete Exam 3 by answering questions 11-20 on pages 53-55. (You should have already answered questions 1-10 as part of your study of lesson 5.)

CHRIST LOVED THE CHURCH

Name_____ Exam Grade_____
(print plainly)

Address _____

City_____ State _____ Zip Code _____ Class Number _____

Instructor _____

LESSON 5

1. List three areas in which the local assembly should seek the guidance of the Holy Spirit. *(5 points)*

a. _____

b. _____

c. _____

In the blank space in the right-hand margin write the letter of the correct answer. (45 points)

2. The Sovereignty of the Spirit means that He
a. is the Head of the church
b. always does things in exactly the same way
c. can and does do as He pleases
d. will only use those who are fully surrendered to Him in every area of their lives
_____

3. The early church was characterized by
a. formalism and ritualism
b. great freedom of the Spirit
c. centralized planning and control
d. a great lack of power
_____

4. In Acts 18:25 and Romans 12:11 the Holy Spirit uses an expression which literally means "to boil." This expression is
a. "full of the Spirit"
b. "baptized with the Spirit"
c. "fervent in Spirit"
d. "on fire for God"
_____

5. Despite its many faults, the Corinthian church was peopled with saints who
   a. never missed a meeting
   b. did all things decently and in order
   c. celebrated the Lord's Supper in a manner which was a living testimony to saint and sinner alike
   d. were aggressively alive to their new life in Christ _____

6. The command "Quench not the Spirit" is addressed primarily to those
   a. living wicked lives
   b. apt to pour cold water on the exuberance of their more effervescent brethren
   c. living in early post-apostolic times
   d. neglecting the truth of the Lord's return _____

7. The most potent thing in the world is
   a. fervor of spirit
   b. wisdom
   c. academic achievement
   d. an orthodox faith _____

8. Which of the gifts is like Aaron's rod in that it seems to swallow up other gifts?
   a. tongues
   b. ruling
   c. preaching
   d. pastoring _____

9. In which of the following situations would one expect the Spirit to be able best to lead? In the situation where
   a. the order of the meeting is prearranged and set in a regular form
   b. the meeting is to close at a specified hour regardless of anything else
   c. no allowance is made for the exercise of gift by brethren in the fellowship, all oral ministry being entrusted to one or two men
   d. human arrangements and rules are at an absolute minimum _____

10. You are in a meeting of the local church convened for worship and for the Lord's Supper. Any brother so led by the Spirit may take part by suggesting a hymn, reading a Scripture passage with or without comment or by leading in prayer. About half way through there is a prolonged silence with no one taking audible part. The spiritual brother would
   a. continue to wait for the Spirit's leading, filling His mind and heart with thoughts of the Lord
   b. give out a hymn to break up the silence
   c. read a passage of Scripture even though he could not find one appropriate to the occasion
   d. pray for those on the mission field since they always need prayer and this would be an appropriate way to end the silence   _____

LESSON 6

In the blank space in the right-hand margin write the letter of the correct answer. (50 points)

11. In the New Testament
   a. church truth is generally found in sections quite separate from sections dealing with personal holiness
   b. church truth is set forth in dogmatic outline form so that it can be clearly grasped and understood
   c. church truth is interwoven with practical instructions for personal godliness of life
   d. church truth is not directly taught at all but has to be inferred from Old Testament typology   _____

12. Sound, systematic teaching of the Word of God
   a. will not altogether eliminate the occasional need for disciplinary action
   b. will render disciplinary action unnecessary
   c. will best be achieved by having a different speaker every Sunday with no regard to where or how the Bible is opened and expounded
   d. is an impossible goal so long as we are still subject to human limitations down here   _____

13. 1 John 2:19 describes
   a. a person who professes to be saved but who is actually unregenerate
   b. a person who introduces the leaven of false teaching into the local gathering of Christians
   c. an assembly of Christians which has lost its first love
   d. an incident of immoral behavior calling for disciplinary action by the local church _____

14. Disciplinary action
   a. has, as its sole function, the cleansing of the local church from contamination with sin
   b. ought to lead ultimately to the recovery of the offender
   c. results in the eternal damnation of the excommunicated believer
   d. should be avoided since it manifests a harsh and un-Christlike spirit in the local assembly _____

15. Which of the following should be deliberately avoided by the members of a local assembly? The person who
   a. falls repeatedly before the power of an ingrained bad habit
   b. owes another brother money and who continually defers payment of his debt
   c. tends to resent the authority of the elders in the local church
   d. causes divisions in order to draw away a following of his own _____

16. A brother in the local assembly announces his disbelief in the virgin birth of Christ. He should be
   a. allowed to continue in the fellowship
   b. immediately excommunicated
   c. given the pulpit to expound his views so that the whole question of the virgin birth can be viewed from every angle
   d. warned twice about his wrong views and then rejected from the fellowship _____

17. When dealing with a case calling for possible disciplinary action the important thing is to
   a. act with all speed, even though the evidence is inconclusive, so as to preserve the purity of the local church
   b. form a judgment only when the evidence of two or three witnesses is forthcoming
   c. give the offender the right to defend himself but take action against him if one reliable witness gives testimony unfavorable to him
   d. take no action at all since people will tend to take sides and cause a division and discord in the local church _____

18. When administering discipline to an erring believer, the elders should do so
    a. authoritatively, emphasizing their position and the prerogatives of their office
    b. apologetically, asking the brother to forgive them for having to take this step
    c. meekly, remembering their own human frailty
    d. dispassionately, taking care to evidence no emotion _____

19. In which of the following cases is it proper to exercise partiality in the matter of church discipline? It is
    a. proper when the guilty party is related to us or to prominent members of the assembly
    b. proper when the guilty party has a winning personality
    c. proper when the guilty party is one of the most influential people in the assembly or community
    d. never proper to exercise partiality _____

20. When a member of the local church has been disciplined it ought to be
    a. kept as secret as possible
    b. published as a news item in the local press
    c. confirmed by letters to all the churches in the area
    d. the end of all future fellowship with this person, come what may _____

WHAT DO YOU SAY?

Do you think the church would be weaker or stronger if it carried out discipline more deliberately? Give a reason for your answer

_____

_____

_____

_____

_____

MAIL TO address shown on back outside cover.
PLEASE enclose a stamped addressed envelope for the return of your corrected exam.

55

Expansion of the Church

Another noteworthy truth concerning the church which the local assembly must put into operation is that gifts are given for the edification of the church. Since edification involves growth or expansion, we are therefore concerned at this point with God's program for the expansion of the church.

The church is the unit on earth today through which God pleases to spread the Christian faith. Each church should always be concerned with spreading out, with reaching new constituencies, with propagating itself, with seeing other assemblies brought into existence.

As has been pointed out previously, the risen Head of the church has provided gifts for the church, and it is as these gifts are properly exercised that the church grows.

GIFTS FOR TODAY

It was mentioned earlier that originally there were five gifts—apostles, prophets, evangelists, pastors, and teachers. It was suggested that the first two were concerned primarily with the foundation of the church, and that, in general, the need for them passed when the complete Word of God was given in written form.

That means that we have three gifts today—evangelists, pastors, and teachers. We turn now to the purpose of the gifts and how they function.

WHY GIFTS ARE GIVEN

The purpose of the gifts is set forth in Ephesians 4:12, 13. "For the perfecting of the saints, for the work of the ministry, for the edifying of the body of Christ: Till we all come in the unity of the faith, and of the knowledge of the Son of God, unto a perfect man, unto the measure of the stature of the fulness of Christ."

Now upon first reading this verse in our King James Version of the Bible, one would think that these are three separate reasons why the gifts were given: namely (1) for the perfecting of the saints, (2) for the work of the ministry, (3) for the edifying of the body of Christ. However, is this what the passage teaches? A study of other versions reveals that it is not.

The Revised Version, for instance, indicates that in the second and third instances of the use of the word "for," the word is better translated "unto." The verse then reads, *"For the perfecting of the saints unto the work of ministering unto the building up of the body of Christ."* This then reveals not three unrelated reasons why the gifts were given, but rather one reason alone—to build up the saints in the faith, *so that they in turn can do the work of ministering* (or serving), so that the body of Christ will be built up numerically and spiritually. It is the saints who are to do the work of ministering.

THE TRUTH ILLUSTRATED

We might illustrate this truth by a diagram. The circle in the center depicts, let us say, the gift of a teacher. He ministers to those in the circle around him, so that they become perfected (that is, built up in the faith), and they then go forth to minister to others. In this way the church grows and expands. It is the divine method of reaching the greatest number of people in the shortest possible time.

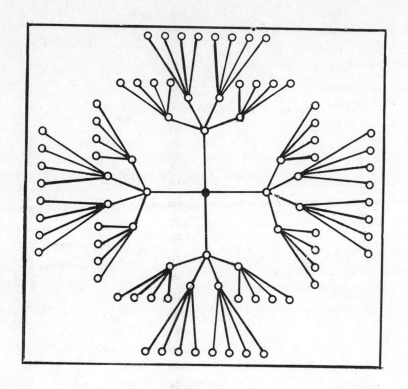

According to this divine pattern, the evangelists and pastors and teachers always have in view the idea of reaching, training, and equipping others to do the work of ministering.

Although not every Christian has the gift of an evangelist, a pastor, or a teacher, yet every one is expected to engage in Christian service. Every member of the church should be a worshipper, a soul winner, a Bible student, a propagator of the faith.

This important obligation is further stressed in 2 Timothy 2:2. "And the things that thou hast heard of me among many witnesses, the same commit thou to faithful men, who shall be able to teach others also."

Once again this can be illustrated by a diagram:

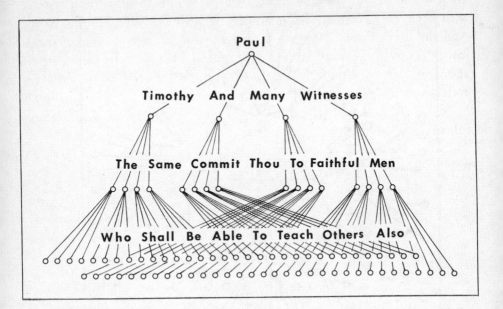

Now this plan produces benefits that are apparent at once. It results in a rapid expansion of the Christian faith. Individual Christians become mature through exercising their God-given functions. By thus becoming mature, they are less susceptible to the teachings of the false cults so current in the world today. And the church thus expanding and maturing gives a more accurate representation of the body of Christ upon earth.

THE SYSTEM COMMON TO CHRISTENDOM

Contrast with this, the system which is so common in Christendom today. One man is selected as minister of a church. He preaches the sermons, baptizes the converts, conducts the communion service, and otherwise performs the religious duties of the congregation. The people listen to the sermons faithfully week after week, but in an unfortunately large number of cases, would be quite unwilling to assume any active participation, reasoning that they are paying someone else to do this for them. They become, in short, professional sermon-tasters, with little real personal acquaintance with the truths of God's Word. And the ever-present danger is that these people, reared in an evangelical environment, remain mere "children, tossed to and fro, and carried about with every wind of doctrine, by the sleight of men, and cunning craftiness, whereby they lie in wait to deceive" (Ephesians 4:14).

The present system we are speaking about may be illustrated as follows:

```
                    Clergyman

                        o


                   Congregation

   o  o  o  o              o  o  o  o

   o  o  o  o              o  o  o  o

   o  o  o  o              o  o  o  o

   o  o  o  o              o  o  o  o
```

Here the minister has his congregation and they dutifully attend the services; but having done so, they go back to their occupations, feeling little or no personal responsibility to do anything about what they have heard. Obviously what one minister can do in such a situation is very limited. On the other hand, if all those people were active for the Lord, the progress would be remarkable.

It was such considerations that caused Alexander Maclaren to write: "I cannot but believe that the present practice of confining the public teaching of the church to an official class has done harm. Why should one man be for ever speaking, and hundreds of people who are able to teach, sitting dumb to listen or pretend to listen to him? I hate forcible revolution, and do not believe that any institutions, either political or ecclesiastical, which need violence to sweep them away, are ready to be removed; but I believe that if the level of spiritual life were raised among us, new forms would naturally be evolved, in which there should be a more adequate recognition of the great principle on which the democracy of Christianity is founded: namely, "I will pour out My Spirit on all flesh—and on My servants and on My handmaidens I will pour out in these days of My Spirit, and they shall prophesy."[1]

THE CLERICAL SYSTEM EXAMINED

This discussion of one-man ministry brings to the front the questions, "What about the clerical system? Is it scriptural?" We shall now seek an answer to these pertinent queries.

By the clergy we mean a separate class of men humanly ordained to the service of God, and usually given sole authority to perform the rites and ordinances of the church.

At the outset we would gladly recognize that many men who have held the clerical position have been outstanding servants of Christ and have been wonderfully used of Him. To many of them and their ministry, both oral and written, we owe a profound debt of gratitude which we gladly acknowledge. All such who are believers in the Lord Jesus, we readily embrace as our brethren.

But we must face honestly and squarely the fact that the idea of a clergyman is not found in the New Testament. Nowhere does one find one man in charge of a church. (At the end of the epistle to Titus, the subscription says, "It was written to Titus, ordained the first bishop of the church of the Cretians, from Nicopolis of Macedonia." However, no one contends that this footnote was part of the original text. It was

---

[1]Maclaren, Alexander, "Colossians and Philemon" in *The Expositor's Bible* (London: Hodder & Stoughton, 1903), pp. 328-330.

added by the translators, who, of course, were biased in favor of clericalism. The Revised Version omits the note altogether.)

WHAT DOES THE NEW TESTAMENT SAY?

Not only is the idea of the clergy unsupported by the New Testament, but, we believe, it is contrary to the teaching of the New Testament.

First of all, it violates the principle of the priesthood of all believers (1 Peter 2:5, 9). In the Old Testament, there was a separate caste of men standing between God and the people. In Christianity, all believers are priests, with all the privileges and responsibilities that go with priesthood. In practice, the idea of a one-man ministry effectively silences the worship and hinders the service of Christian priests.

Secondly, the clerical system prohibits the free exercise of gifts in the church (1 Corinthians 12 and 14), by arbitrarily limiting ministry to one person or an official group of persons.

Again, it confines the administration of the ordinances to a priestly caste, whereas Scripture makes no such distinction.

The principle of salaried ministry, which almost invariably accompanies the clerical system, inevitably involves responsibility to some higher person or persons. This higher authority may exert pressure on a minister by imposing artificial and unspiritual standards of attainment. For instance, it is common to judge a man's effectiveness by the number of persons added to the church roll during the year. Not only is this not a true measure of effective ministry, but it creates the strong temptation to lower the standards of reception in order to make a better showing. The servant of Christ should not thus be bound, fettered, and hampered. He should ever be the Lord's free man (Galatians 1:10).

Clerisy caters to the ever present danger of gathering people to a man instead of to the Name of the Lord. If a man is the attracting power in a local church, then the attraction is gone when the man leaves. If on the other hand the saints gather because the Lord is there, then they will be faithful because of Him.

In practice, if not in theory, the clergy has served to obscure effectively the truth of the headship of Christ (Ephesians 1:22), and

63

in some cases to deny it completely.

If it be contended that the bishops of the New Testament are the same as the clergy of today, we would reply that the New Testament contemplates several bishops in one church (Philippians 1:1), and not one bishop presiding over a church or a group of churches.

It is undeniable that many men in the clerical position are gifted servants of Christ to the church. However, they did not become gifts by human appointment or ordination but by the work of the Lord Jesus Himself. They are responsible to so minister that the saints will be built up for active service, and not so that the saints will become perpetually dependent on them.

The evils that have flowed from human ordination of men who were not called of God are manifest and need no elaboration here.

Finally where one man is primarily responsible for the teaching ministry of the church, there is no system of checks and balances, and thus there is a danger of one-sided interpretations, if not of evil doctrine itself. Where the Holy Spirit, on the other hand, has liberty to speak through various gifts in the church, more facets of the truth are brought to light, and there is greater immunity from error where all the saints are assiduously comparing Scripture with Scripture.

CONCLUSION

Thus, though much blessing has often flowed from the ministry of men representing the clerical system, we believe that it is not only not God's best but that it is seriously detrimental to the best interests of the church.

God's way is for the gifts to minister to the saints, then for the saints in turn to go forth to do the work of the ministry. The local assembly should recognize this important principle, and do nothing to hinder its free development. As the saints thus minister, unbelievers will be saved, saints will be edified, and new assemblies will be brought into being.

Exam questions for lesson 7 will be found on pages 75-77.

Lesson 8

Ordained of God

THE PRIESTHOOD OF BELIEVERS

The seventh and final truth concerning the church which we listed at the outset was that all believers are priests of God. Every local assembly should witness to this truth practically by refusing any other priesthood and by encouraging every believer to exercise the privileges and responsibilities of this sacred office, both individually and collectively.

1. A Contrast

In the Old Testament, the law of Moses set aside the tribe of Levi and the family of Aaron to be the priests of the nation. These men had distinctive dress, were given special privileges, and stood as a separate caste between God and the congregation of Israel. They alone could enter the holy place, and only they could offer the sacrifices prescribed by the law.

In Christianity all this changed. Now all believers are priests, according to the New Testament. 1 Peter 2:5 states, "Ye also, as lively stones, are built up a spiritual house, *an holy priesthood,* to offer up spiritual sacrifices, acceptable to God by Jesus Christ." 1 Peter 2:9 says, "But ye are a chosen generation, *a royal priesthood,* an holy nation, a peculiar people: that ye should show forth the praises of Him who hath called you out of darkness into His marvelous light." Revelation 1:5, 6 declares, "Unto Him that loved us, and washed us from our sins in His own blood, and hath made us kings and *priests* unto God and His Father; to Him be glory and dominion for ever and ever. Amen."

Martin Luther earnestly contended for the truth of the priesthood of all believers. He wrote: "All believers are altogether priests, and let it be anathema to assert that there is any other priest than he who is Christian; for it will be asserted without the Word of God, on no authority but the sayings of men, or the antiquity of custom, or the multitude of those that think so."[1]

2. Our Sacrifices

Among the important duties of a priest is that of offering sacrifice. In the Old Testament the sacrifices usually consisted of slain animals. Today, a believer offers the sacrifice of his body (Romans 12:1). This is not a dead offering, but "a living sacrifice, holy, acceptable unto God." He also offers his material resources (Hebrews 13:16). "But to do good and to communicate forget not: for with such sacrifices God is well pleased."

Then, too, there is the sacrifice of praise (Hebrews 13:15). "By Him therefore let us offer the sacrifice of praise to God continually, that is, the fruit of our lips giving thanks unto His Name." This sacrifice of praise should be both individual and collective. The latter—collective worship—in which believers are at liberty to take part in public praise has been practically eliminated by the stereotyped, controlled services of our day. The result is a generation of dumb priests—a state of affairs nowhere contemplated in the Scriptures.

3. Other Priestly Duties

Other duties of a priest include prayer, testimony for God, and care for His people. Thus, believers should continually be exercising this sacred office. Eric Sauer says: "The teaching of all

---

[1]Quoted by Hoste, W., *Bishops, Priests and Deacons* (London: Pickering & Inglis, n.d.), p. 73.

Scripture on this subject (Romans 8:14; Galatians 5:18; John 16: 13), makes clear that it has to be applied to our whole life from morning till evening, and every day in the week, not only the Lord's Day. It is certainly not limited to the beginning and ending of church gatherings, such as meetings for worship, Bible reading, or prayer, but includes the whole man, not only in but also outside the meeting-rooms, halls, chapels, and church buildings. In this full sense of the word the whole New Testament people of God is 'a kingdom of priests and a holy nation' (Exodus 19:6; 1 Peter 2:5-9)."[1]

4. Our Great High Priest

Although it is true that all believers are priests, it is also true that every Christian needs a priest. He finds that need fully met in the Lord Jesus Christ. The Epistle to the Hebrews sets forth that blessed One as the Great High Priest, One who can be touched with the feeling of our infirmities because He was in all points tempted like as we are, yet without sin (Hebrews 4:15).

5. What Christendom Has Done

Every local church then should recognize the Lord Jesus as the Great High Priest, and every believer as an holy and royal priest. But is this what we find in Christendom today? On the contrary, we find that the church has gone back to the priestly system of Judaism. While professing to believe in the priesthood of all Christians, many churches have set up a distinct priesthood of their own, based largely on the Mosaic system. Thus we have a separate class of men set apart for divine service, a hierarchy of church officials with highsounding titles that distinguish them from the laity, and distinctive garb to set these men apart as being of a different order. In addition, the church has borrowed from Judaism such concepts as consecrated buildings with their elaborate altars,

[1] Sauer, Erich, *In the Arena of Faith* (Grand Rapids: Wm. B. Eerdmans Publ. Co., 1955), p. 134.

ecclesiastical adornments, and material aids to worship, an impressive ritual that appeals to the natural senses, and a religious calendar with its holy days and seasons.

Concerning this atrocious mixture of Judaism and Christianity, Dr. C. I. Scofield commented: "It may safely be said that the Judaizing of the church has done more to hinder her progress, pervert her mission, and destroy her spirituality, than all other causes combined. Instead of pursuing her appointed path of separation from the world and following the Lord in her heavenly calling, she has used Jewish Scriptures to justify herself in lowering her purpose to the civilization of the world, the acquisition of wealth, the use of an imposing ritual, the erection of magnificent churches, the invocation of God's blessing upon the conflicts of armies, and the division of an equal brotherhood into 'clergy' and 'laity.' "[1]

6. What Should Be Done?

Is not God calling upon His people today to separate themselves from this religion of types and shadows, in order that they might find their sufficiency in the Name of the Lord Jesus?

Only such a church is fully realizing its share in the New Testament general priesthood which is, to quote Erich Sauer, "A local church with Spirit-filled, regularly well-attended prayer meetings;

"A local church with members who are practical helpers and fellow-workers with the Lord's servants in the world-wide harvest field;

"A local church with persevering, energetic activity in the preaching of the Gospel, by tract distribution, personal witness, and, wherever possible, open-air meetings;

"A local church with a warm-hearted, spiritual atmosphere of love, where everyone tries to help the other by mutual care and

---

[1] Scofield, Dr. C. I., *Rightly Dividing the Word of Truth* (New York: Loizeaux Bros., Inc., n.d.), p. 17.

charity in a prayerful spirit, considering one another to provoke unto love and good works.

"In such a local church the gatherings and services also will be under the guidance of the Holy Spirit, and the gifts of the Holy Spirit, as distributed by the Lord Himself, will be developed in their God-appointed variety, in brotherly fellowship, in dependence upon Christ, and thus in holy freedom of the Spirit (1 Corinthians 12:4-11; 14:26). And when the church is gathered together at the Lord's Table praising the priestly sacrifice on Golgotha, priestly worship will rise up to the heavenly Sanctuary, thus crowning the privilege of the general priesthood of the church."[1]

7. Looking Ahead

With this section on priesthood, we bring to a close our study of seven vital truths concerning the universal church which every local church should seek to portray and practice. Needless to say, other truths could be mentioned, but these are sufficient to show that the assembly should be a replica or miniature of all that is true of the entire body of Christ. In the pages to follow we shall deal with the ordinances of the church, the prayer meeting, the bishops and deacons, the finances of the church, and the ministry of women. There will be a concluding lesson entitled, "Let Us Go Forth Unto Him!"

BAPTISM

The two ordinances of the Christian church are baptism and the Lord's Supper. We find these instituted in the Gospels (Matthew 28:19; Luke 22:19, 20); practiced in the Acts (Chapter 10:47, 48; 20:7); and expounded in the Epistles (Romans 6:3-10; 1 Corinthians 11:23-32).[2]

---

[1] Sauer, op. cit., pp. 151, 152.

[2] For a complete study of baptism the student should take the Emmaus course *Buried by Baptism.*

1. Three Baptisms

In considering the subject of baptism, we should notice at the outset that there are three main forms of baptism in the New Testament.

First of all, there is the baptism of John (Mark 1:4). As the forerunner of the coming King, John called upon the nation of Israel to repent and to bring forth fruits worthy of repentance (Matthew 3:8). Those who came to him, confessing their sins, were baptized unto repentance, and they thus separated themselves from the ungodly condition of the nation. The Lord Jesus was baptized by John, not because He had sins of which to repent, but in order to identify Himself with the repentant remnant of Israel, and fulfill all righteousness (Matthew 3:15).

Secondly, there is believer's baptism (Romans 6:3, 4). This signifies identification with Christ in His death, and will be discussed in detail later.

Thirdly, there is the baptism of the Holy Spirit (1 Corinthians 12:13). This is the sovereign work of the Spirit of God by which all who believe on the Savior are incorporated into the body of Christ.

2. Significant Contrasts

In connection with these three baptisms, it should be carefully noted that John's baptism is not the same as Spirit baptism. These are clearly distinguished in Matthew 3:11. John's baptism is not the same as believer's baptism. Acts 19:1-5 shows that those who were already baptized as John's disciples had to be rebaptized with Christian baptism. *The baptism of the Holy Spirit is not the same as believer's baptism. Many have a vague idea that water baptism is a picture or portrayal of Spirit baptism. Actually they are entirely distinct.* Spirit baptism speaks of incorporation into Christ's body, whereas believer's baptism is a type of death. In short, all these three forms of baptism are different, and should not be confused.

70

3. Believer's Baptism

There is no mention in the New Testament, after the day of Pentecost, of any persons being baptized except those who were believers in the Lord Jesus. Note the following—"Then they that gladly received his word were baptized" (Acts 2:41). "When they believed Philip preaching the things concerning the kingdom of God, and the name of Jesus Christ, they were baptized, both men and women" (Acts 8:12). It is true that households are mentioned as being baptized (Acts 16:15; 1 Corinthians 1:16); but there is no evidence to suppose that these households included children who had never trusted the Lord Jesus.

4. The Significance of It

The principal meaning of believer's baptism is most fully developed in Romans 6:1-10. We might summarize the teaching of that passage as follows. When Jesus died, He went, as it were, under the waves and billows of God's wrath (Psalm 42:7). He did this as our Representative. Because Christ really died in our place, we can say that when He died, we died. By dying, He settled the whole question of sin once and for all. Therefore, we too have died to the whole question of sin. Sin no longer has any claim on us. God sees every believer as having been crucified with Christ. All that he was as a sinner in the flesh has been nailed to the cross. In baptism, the believer gives a dramatic illustration of what has already taken place. In going under the water, he is saying in effect, "Because of my sins, I deserved to die. But when Jesus died, I died too. My old man, or old self, was crucified with Him. When Jesus was buried, I too was buried, and I now acknowledge that my old self should be put away from God's sight forever as a matter of daily practice." Then just as Jesus arose from the dead, so the believer arises out of the waters of baptism. In so doing, he signifies his determination to walk in newness of life. No longer will he live to please self, but rather he will turn over his life to the Savior so that He can live His life in the believer.

Thus we might say that baptism is an ordinance signifying the end of the former way of life. It is a public act of obedience to the will of the Lord (Matthew 28:19, 20), picturing the believer's death with Christ. It has no saving merit, but is for those who are already saved.

5. The Method

Endless controversy has arisen over the question as to how baptism should be administered—whether by sprinkling or by immersion. The following facts are helpful in seeking a solution. The word "baptize" comes from a Greek word meaning "to dip, plunge, wash." In connection with the baptism of Christ, we read, "And Jesus, when He was baptized, went up straightway *out of the water"* (Matthew 3:16). John himself was baptizing in Aenon, near to Salim, "because there was *much water there"* (John 3:23). At the baptism of the Ethiopian eunuch, the Scripture is careful in noting that "they went down both *into the water,* both Philip and the eunuch; and he baptized him. And when they were come up *out of the water,* the Spirit of the Lord caught away Philip . . ." (Acts 8:38, 39). We saw above (Romans 6:3) that baptism is a likeness or picture of burial. Sprinkling does not convey any likeness of burial, whereas immersion does so most accurately.

6. The Important Thing

But even more important than the mode of baptism is the heart condition of the person being baptized. There are thousands of persons who have been immersed in water, but who have not been really baptized. The truly baptized person is the one who has not only gone through the outward ordinance, but whose life shows that the flesh, or old nature, has been put in the place of death. Baptism must be a matter of the heart, as well as an outward profession.

This may be expressed rather pointedly by paraphrasing Romans 2:25-29 to refer to baptism instead of circumcision.

"Baptism indeed profiteth if thou be an obeyer of the Gospel; but if thou be a refuser of a Gospel-walk, then baptism is become non-baptism. If, therefore, an un-baptized person obeys the Gospel, shall not his non-baptism be reckoned for baptism? And shall not unbaptized persons, if they obey the Gospel, judge thee, who with the letter and baptism, art a refuser of a Gospel-walk. For he is not a Christian who is one outwardly, nor is that baptism which is outward in the flesh; but he is a Christian who is one inwardly, and baptism is that of the heart, in the spirit, not in the letter, whose praise is not of men but of God."[1]

7. Administering the Rite

The idea that a man must be an ordained minister in order to baptize is unscriptural. Any man who is a believer may baptize others.

COUNTING THE COST

In the early days of the church, when a believer was baptized, he was often persecuted and murdered in a short time. Yet whenever others were saved, they unhesitatingly stepped forward to fill up the ranks of the martyrs by being baptized.

Even today in certain areas, baptism is often the signal for the beginning of terrible persecution. In many countries, a believer is tolerated as long as he only confesses Christ with his lips. But whenever he publicly confesses Christ in baptism and severs his ties with the past, the enemies of the cross take up their battle against him.

Yet whatever the cost may be, each one who is baptized enjoys the same experience as the Ethiopian eunuch, of whom it is written, "He went on his way rejoicing."

---

[1] Suggested by a similar paraphrase on church-membership by Newell, Wm. R., *Romans, Verse by Verse* (Chicago: Grace Publications, 1945), p. 70.

When you are ready, complete Exam 4 by answering questions 10-19 on pages 77-79. (You should have already answered questions 1-9 as part of your study of lesson 7.)

CHRIST LOVED THE CHURCH

Exam
Name_____Grade_____
(print plainly)

Address _____

City_____ State _____ Zip
Code _____ Class
Number _____

Instructor _____

LESSON 7

In the blank space in the right-hand margin write the letter of the correct answer. (40 points)

1. God is pleased today to spread the Christian faith through the instrumentality of
   a. angels who further His cause in ways unknown to men
   b. the church to which the Lord has given appropriate gifts
   c. independent organizations which, in God's view, are far more efficient than the local church
   d. the Holy Spirit who works independently of the church   _____

2. Ephesians 4:12, 13 (in the Revised Version)
   a. gives three separate reasons why gifts are given to the church
   b. gives one reason why God has given gifts to the church
   c. gives warrant for concentrating the work of ministering into the hands of one man in the local church
   d. gives scriptural authority for the setting up of evangelistic organizations outside the fellowship of the church   _____

3. Which of the following Scriptures best supports the teaching of Ephesians 4:12, 13?
   a. Romans 10:14
   b. 1 Corinthians 3:5
   c. Philippians 1:1
   d. 2 Timothy 2:2   _____

4. The clergy/laity system, so common in Christendom, is weak in that it often

a. breeds professional sermon tasters

b. saps at the desire of the congregation at large to engage in the spiritual and outreach functions of the local church

c. retards spiritual development in the "laity"

d. does all the above _____

5. The subscription at the end of the epistle to Titus

a. was written by Paul but was not inspired

b. proves that the idea of a clergy is scriptural

c. is not a part of the original inspired text

d. really belongs at the end of the Epistle to Timothy _____

6. The idea of a clergy conflicts with the scriptural teaching of

a. the priesthood of all believers

b. the oneness of the body

c. the separation of church and state

d. the baptism of the Spirit _____

7. The idea that the bishops of the New Testament are the same as the clergy of today is contradicted by the fact that

a. New Testament bishops were ordained by the apostles themselves

b. in New Testament times there was a plurality of bishops in any given local church

c. the word "bishops" as used in the New Testament was only applied to those who had been priests in the Jewish religion

d. New Testament bishops were hereditary and fell heir to their office only upon the death of a lineal predecessor _____

8. Checks and balances to counter one-sided interpretations in a local church function best

a. where all believers can share in the spoken ministry of the assembly as the Spirit leads

b. when one man, trained in theology in a recognized seminary, takes charge of the oral ministry

c. when a central headquarters issues written "lessons" to be read to local congregations

d. when the teaching from a given pulpit is periodically checked by overseers from a central Board charged with keeping the teaching true to Scripture _____

9. Give two diagrams in the spaces provided below. One diagram should illustrate the generally accepted clergy/laity system. The other diagram should illustrate the system envisioned in the New Testament. *(10 points)*

The Clergy/Laity System	The New Testament System

LESSON 8

10. List 3 features of the Old Testament priesthood which do not apply to the church. *(5 points)*

a. _____

b. _____

c. _____

11. Give one Scripture reference taken from the lesson, which proves that all believers are priests. *(5 points)*

_____

In the blank space in the right-hand margin write the letter of the correct answer. (40 points)

12. The sacrifices of a New Testament priest include
    a. yielding his body to God
    b. surrendering his money for God to use
    c. taking part in audible public praise
    d. all the above
    e. none of the above

    _____

77

13. Which of the following Scriptures tells who is The Great High Priest for believers today?
    a. 1 Corinthians 4:1
    b. Hebrews 5:1-4
    c. Hebrews 4:14, 15
    d. Revelation 22:8   _____

14. According to Scofield the church's habit of mixing Judaism with Christianity has
    a. been a great help to the church in its ministry
    b. been a somewhat mixed blessing for the church
    c. stimulated greatly the course of antisemitism
    d. provoked the Jews to jealousy as Paul predicted
    e. hindered the progress of the church, perverted her mission and destroyed her spirituality   _____

15. The Lord left with His church
    a. only two ordinances
    b. a large number of ordinances
    c. no ordinance at all, baptism and the Lord's Supper really being sacraments
    d. two ordinances and three sacraments   _____

16. Which of the following statements is erroneous?
    a. John's baptism and Christian baptism serve similar functions
    b. believer's baptism is a picture or portrayal of Spirit baptism
    c. the baptism of the Holy Spirit identifies the believer with Christ in His death, burial and resurrection
    d. all the above are erroneous   _____

17. Which of the following is *NOT* true of believer's baptism as the subject is developed in Romans 6:1-10?
    a. In baptism we are identified with Christ in His death
    b. In baptism the believer gives to the world an illustration of what has already taken place in his life
    c. Baptism is the outward expression of an inward experience
    d. Water baptism is necessary for salvation   _____

18. Acts 8:38, 39 implies that
    a. it is scriptural to baptize infants
    b. sprinkling is an acceptable mode of baptism
    c. baptism in New Testament times was by immersion
    d. only an ordained minister can properly baptize   _____

78

19. The important thing in baptism is
   a. the qualifications of the person performing the rite
   b. the site where the baptism takes place
   c. the heart condition of the person being baptized
   d. all the above _____

WHAT DO YOU SAY?

How would you counsel someone who told you he was a genuine believer but was afraid to be baptized because he would be persecuted for it at home?

_____

_____

_____

_____

_____

Lesson 9

Coming to God

THE LORD'S SUPPER

This solemn act of remembrance was instituted by the Lord Jesus on the night of His betrayal.[1] Immediately after He had celebrated the last Passover with His disciples, He introduced what we know as the Lord's supper. "He took bread, and gave thanks, and brake it, and gave unto them, saying, 'This is my body which is given for you: this do in remembrance of me.' Likewise also the cup after supper, saying, 'This cup is the new testament in my blood, which is shed for you' " (Luke 22:19, 20).

1. Why Keep the Feast?

With regard to the significance of this ordinance, certain facts are presented. First, it is an occasion for remembrance. The Savior said, "This do in remembrance of Me." It is a time to remember His sufferings and death, the giving of His body, the shedding of His blood. Here Calvary with all its sacred associations passes before the minds of the participants. It is quite impossible thus to remember the passion of the Lord Jesus without responding to God with worship and praise. Thus the Lord's supper is a time of

---

[1] For a complete study of the remembrance feast the student should take the Emmaus course *The Lord's Supper.*

public worship, a time of adoring God for all He is and all He has done.

Then again, the Lord's supper is a public witness to the unity of the body of Christ. The loaf of bread is a picture of the body of Christ, made up of all true believers. In partaking of the bread, the believer testifies that he is one with every true child of God. In drinking of the cup, he acknowledges that he is one with everyone who has been cleansed by the precious blood (1 Corinthians 10:16, 17).

Finally, the Lord's supper is a constant reminder that the One who instituted this memorial of Himself is coming again. "For as often as ye eat this bread and drink this cup, ye do show the Lord's death till He come" (1 Corinthians 11:26). Thus, the worshipper not only looks back to Golgotha and remembers Him in His death, he not only looks upward to the Throne of God and praises Him for an accomplished redemption, but he also looks forward to that moment when the Lord will descend from heaven and take His waiting people home.

2. As Oft As Ye Do

With regard to the time and frequency of the Lord's supper, the Scriptures do not command in the language of law, but entreat with the voice of grace. In Acts 20:7, it is stated that "upon the first day of the week, . . . the disciples came together to break bread." The first day of the week is the Lord's Day, or Sunday. It is the day of the Lord's resurrection and a fitting day for His people to meet together for worship and remembrance. The instruction is, "As often as ye eat this bread and drink this cup" (1 Corinthians 11:26). The moment a person says it *must* be observed every week, or month, or quarter, he has gone beyond what the Bible says. At the same time, the probability is very strong that the early disciples met every week to remember the Lord.

Charles Haddon Spurgeon argued strongly for a weekly observance of the Lord's supper. "My witness is, and I think I speak the mind of many of God's people now present, that coming as some of us do, weekly, to the Lord's Table, we do not find the breaking of bread to have lost its significance—it is always fresh to us. I have often remarked on Lord's day evening, whatever the subject may have been, whether Sinai has thundered over our heads, or the plaintive notes of Calvary have pierced our hearts, it always seems equally appropriate to come to the breaking of bread. Shame on the Christian church that she should put it off to once a month, and mar the first day of the week by depriving it of its glory in the meeting together for fellowship and breaking of bread, and showing forth the death of Christ till He come. They who once know the sweetness of each Lord's day celebrating His supper will not be content, I am sure, to put it off to less frequent seasons."[1]

Jonathan Edwards also was an advocate of a weekly remembrance of the Lord. "It seems plain by the Scripture, that the primitive Christians were wont to celebrate this memorial of the sufferings of their dear Redeemer every Lord's Day, and so I believe it will be again in the church of Christ in days that are approaching."[2]

3.   Eligibility

It should scarcely need to be mentioned that the Lord's supper is only for Christians. Only those who have been redeemed are eligible and capable of entering into its sacred meaning. Christians themselves should partake of the emblems in a judged condition (1 Corinthians 11:28). Sin must be confessed and forsaken, and the emblems must be taken in a worthy manner (1 Corinthians 11: 21, 22). All who partake without judging themselves are in danger of being chastened by the Lord (1 Corinthians 11:27, 29-32).

Here again it is good to remind ourselves that it is possible to eat the bread and drink the wine without really remembering the Lord. It is possible to reduce this ordinance to a mere ritual if our

---

[1] Spurgeon, C. H., *Treasury of the Old Testament* (London: Marshall, Morgan & Scott), Vol. I, p. 543.
[2] *Thoughts on Revival*, 1736 (Details unknown).

heart does not answer to what we are doing in symbol. Our lives must be in fellowship with God if we are truly to obey His words, "Remember me."

THE PRAYER MEETING

Not very much information is given in the New Testament concerning the meetings of the local church. We do know that the Christians assembled for fellowship, prayer, ministry of the Word, and breaking of bread (Acts 2:42); but beyond that there seems to be a veil. As far as gospel testimony is concerned, that appears to have been carried on by the individual Christian outside the confines of the assembly, wherever the unsaved could be reached, but always with the idea of bringing the ones who were saved into the fellowship of a local church.

Of all the gatherings of the early assemblies, certainly none was more prominent than the prayer meeting. In fact, the church was born in the wake of a prayer meeting (Acts 1:14), and thereafter the Christians "continued stedfastly in prayer" (Acts 2:42). Indeed, the entire history of the church is a tribute to the faithfulness of God who answers prayer.

1.   A Special Promise

We do well to remind ourselves constantly that collective prayer not only has divine sanction, but carries with it a special promise of the presence of the Lord Himself. In Matthew 18:19 and 20, we read, "Again I say unto you, That if two of you shall agree on earth as touching any thing that they shall ask, it shall be done for them of my Father which is in heaven. For where two or three are gathered together in my name, there am I in the midst of them." Now language could scarcely be clearer than this. We have a two-fold pledge that cannot be broken. First, when two believers are united in presenting a petition to God, that request is answered. Secondly, when Christians are gathered in the Name of the Lord Jesus, He is there in their midst. The trouble is that we do not believe it. If we did, our prayer meetings would be filled, and our churches would be on fire for God.

2. How to Pray as a Group

In considering the subject of collective prayer, we should like at the outset to present a few elementary facts concerning it. First of all, in a prayer meeting, one person leads at a time. The others are silent, but actually all are praying. The one whose voice is audible is expressing the prayers of the group. The others follow him as he prays, and makes his prayer their own. Oftentimes they express this unity of spirit by saying "Amen." Next, we want to mention that there is a big difference between "saying prayers" and praying. There is a children's hymn which makes this distinction:

> I often say my prayers
> But do I ever pray?
> And do the wishes of my heart
> Go with the words I say?
>
> I may as well kneel down
> And worship gods of stone
> As offer to the living God
> A prayer of words alone.
>
> For words without the heart
> The Lord will never hear;
> Nor will He to those lips attend
> Whose prayers are not sincere.[1]

There is nothing that will kill a prayer meeting more quickly than a series of rehearsed prayers where there is no real heart interest. Too often we just go through a list of empty petitions, and the prayers bounce back from the ceiling. The prayers of young converts are usually refreshing because they are spontaneous and fresh. But older Christians frequently fall into a pattern of prayer

---

[1] Burton, J., Poem, *Do I Ever Pray?*

that is useless for God or man. It has been well said, "Meetings where prayers are offered from a sense of duty only, need closing down."[1]

Another danger that should be avoided is long prayers. It is true that Scripture says "Pray without ceasing," but this does not authorize an individual to monopolize the time in the prayer meeting. If the prayers are short and many different men take part, the interest will be increased.

Then, too, our requests should be specific. Do not pray, "God, save many souls throughout the world." Better pray, "Lord, save my brother, David." Then when David is saved, you will know your prayer has been answered and you will be encouraged to pray for others by name.

3.   Be Specific

There is no reason why any prayer meeting should be a dull affair. There are plenty of specific requests which we can bring to the Throne of Grace. Here are a few of them.

Pray for those who are in authority over us, mentioning them by name. Pray that they might be saved, and that we might lead a quiet and peaceable life in all godliness and honesty (1 Timothy 2:2).

Pray for those who are sick in your church. The Lord knows who they are, but maybe some of the Christians don't, so give their names.

Pray for unsaved relatives and friends. We should never be ashamed to have our loved ones mentioned in the prayer meeting. If we really want them to be saved, we will welcome the prayer support of the church.

Pray for the elders in the church. They have important responsibilities which require wisdom and patience. They deserve an interest in your supplications.

Pray for missionaries who have gone out from your assembly.

---

[1] Fisk, E. G., *The Prickly Pear* (London: Marshall, Morgan & Scott, 1951), p. 126.

If you correspond with them from time to time, you will know what problems they are facing and what their needs might be.

Pray for the Sunday School, for its superintendent, for the teachers, and for the boys and girls who are being taught the Word of God.

Pray for the poor. If it would cause embarrassment to anyone present, it might be better to withhold names in this instance.

Pray for the men and women from your assembly in the armed forces. They face dangers, temptations and trials. They need your prayers.

Pray for those who are engaged in the work of the Lord, such as evangelists and teachers.

Then in your prayers be sure to include thanksgiving. This is forcefully brought before us in Philippians 4:6. "Be careful for nothing; but in every thing by prayer and supplication *with thanksgiving* let your requests be made known unto God."

The Lord rightfully expects His people to be thankful. Ingratitude for all His mercies is sin.

4. Important Conditions

But are there not conditions that must be observed if our prayers are to be answered? Indeed there are!

First, we must abide in Christ. He said, "If ye abide in me, and my words abide in you, ye shall ask what ye will, and it shall be done unto you" (John 15:7). Abiding in Christ is keeping His commandments, doing His will, obeying His Word.

Secondly, our prayers should be according to His will. "And this is the confidence that we have in Him, that, if we ask anything according to His will, He heareth us" (1 John 5:14). Since the general outline of God's will is found in the Bible, our requests should be scriptural.

Third, our requests should be offered in the Name of Christ. "And whatsoever ye shall ask in My Name, that will I do, that the Father may be glorified in the Son" (John 14:13). "Whatsoever ye shall ask the Father in My Name, He will give it you" (John

16:23). When we truly ask in His Name, it is the same as if He were making the request to God.

Finally, our motives must be pure. James reminds us that we ask and receive not because we ask amiss, that we may consume it upon our lusts (James 4:3). If our motives are selfish and sinful, we cannot expect an answer.

5. A Few Rules to Remember

Now before we close, there are a few more do's and don't's which should be mentioned if our prayer meetings are going to be "the power-house of the church." For instance, do not pray to be seen. The hypocrites, you remember, love to stand praying in the corners of the streets that they may be seen of men (Matthew 6:5). Again, do not ask God to do something you can do yourself. We ask God to bring the unsaved into our Gospel meetings. Does He not expect us to use our lips to invite them and our cars to bring them? And be careful that you do not ask for something you know you should not have. God sometimes grants such requests but sends leanness to the soul (Psalm 106:15). Do not be discouraged if the answer does not come immediately. God's answers are never too early lest we miss the blessedness of waiting upon Him; they are never too late lest we fear we have trusted Him in vain. Then, if God's answer is not just exactly what you asked for, remember this! The Lord reserves the right to give us something better than we ask for. We do not know what is best for us, but He does, and so He gives us more than we could ever ask or think.

Now let us emphasize in closing that there can be no real progress in the church without prayer. We can go through a routine, and produce even seeming results, but nothing is accomplished for God apart from intercession. If we do not see this conclusion from the Scriptures, we will be soon driven to it by sheer necessity.

Exam questions for lesson 9 will be found on pages 97-99.

Lesson 10

The Bishops

No discussion of the church would be complete without consideration of God's provision for its spiritual care and oversight. We shall find that this work is performed by those known as bishops or elders. At the very outset, we shall want to be clear on several points.

WHAT IS A BISHOP?

First of all, we must distinguish between the New Testament concept of a bishop, and the title as it is used today. In the apostolic church, a bishop was simply one of several mature Christians in a local church who cared for the spiritual welfare of that church. Today, in church systems, a bishop is an appointed dignitary who has many churches under his jurisdiction. Barnes says: "The word *bishop* in the New Testament never means what is now commonly understood by it—a *Prelate*. It does not denote here (i.e. ih 1 Timothy 3) or anywhere else in the New Testament, one who has charge over a diocese composed of a certain district of country embracing a number of churches with their clergy."[1]

In the New Testament, the bishops were not a class of men, mediating between God and man. Perhaps it was as a rebuke to such

---

[1] Barnes, Albert, *Notes on the New Testament* (London: Blackie & Son, No date), Vol. VIII, p. 155.

pretension as might arise in the future that the Spirit of God listed the bishops second, not first, when Paul wrote to the church at Philippi, "To all the saints in Christ Jesus . . . with the bishops and deacons."

In the New Testament, the thought of officialism is absent. Instead of a lofty office with magnificent titles, we are pointed to humble service among the people of God. Thus we read, "If any one is eager for oversight, he is desirous of a *good work.*"[1] Overseership is work, not dignity of office.

Finally, we would notice, by way of introduction, that the words, "bishop," "elder," "overseer," and "presbyter" all refer to the same person in the New Testament. This can be demonstrated by the following comparisons of Scripture with Scripture. In Acts 20:17, we find a reference made to the "elders" of the church. The margin of the Revised Version indicates that this word is the same as "presbyters." Then in Acts 20:28, these same "elders" or "presbyters" are called "overseers." Here the word "overseers" is translated "bishops" in the Revised Version. In Titus 1:5, Paul instructs Titus to ordain "elders"; he then immediately (v. 7) proceeds to give the qualifications of a "bishop," indicating again that "elders" are the same as "bishops."

HOW BISHOPS ARE SELECTED

Now let us consider the question of how elders are selected or appointed. In the final analysis, only the Holy Spirit can make a man an elder (Acts 20:28). A church may meet in solemn session to appoint elders, but their vote does not put within a man the heart of an overseer. The scriptural order would seem to be that God makes men overseers, then as they carry on their work, the church recognizes them as divinely-appointed bishops.

If it be argued that Paul and others appointed bishops (Acts 14:23; Titus 1:5), we would simply say that this was before the New Testament was available in written form in the churches. In the absence of

---

[1] Translation of 1 Timothy 3:1 by Kelly, Wm., *An Exposition of Timothy* (London: C. A. Hammond), p. 57.

written instructions as to the qualifications of elders, the churches had to depend on these apostles or apostolic delegates. It should also be noted that Paul never ordained elders on his first visit to a church. Rather he allowed time for those elders whom God had ordained to manifest themselves by their work. Then he singled them out for recognition by the church.

THE QUALIFICATIONS OF A BISHOP

The Scriptures leave us in no doubt as to the qualifications of a true bishop or elder. These are found in 1 Timothy 3:1-7 and in Titus 1:6-9.

First of all, the bishop must be blameless. As to his reputation, he must be above reproach. It does not say he must be sinless, but blameless. If a public accusation can be proved against a man, he should refrain from assuming the duties of an overseer.

Secondly, he must be the husband of one wife. Some understand this to mean that he must be a married man. Others see in it a prohibition against a polygamist ever becoming an elder. We can definitely say that the latter is true, but it is hard to be dogmatic on the first.

Next, he must be vigilant. The Revised Version tells that this means temperate. He must not be a man given to excess. Some persons find it hard to be moderate. They are always going to extremes. Such men may be in the church, but they may not be overseers.

The elder must be sober, or sober-minded. He must evidence by his life that Christianity is not a pleasant pastime, a frivolous trifle. The elder grapples with eternal issues.

He must be of good behavior, or a better rendering would be "orderly." Carelessness or slip-shod methods are unbecoming to one who would serve in a house of order.

Next, we read, "given to hospitality," or "a lover of hospitality." His home should be open to the Lord's people. It should be like the home of Lazarus, Mary and Martha in Bethany—a place where Jesus loved to be.

The bishop should be apt to teach. Although he might not be an outstandingly gifted teacher, still he should be sufficiently proficient

91

in handling the Scriptures to be able to help the people of God with problems as they arise.

He must not be addicted to wine, or as another translation renders it, he must not be a brawler. The two are closely allied. Any man who cannot control his own appetite surely is not worthy of a place of trust in the church.

He must not be a striker. The literal meaning is that he must not use violence on others. To strike a servant, for instance, would be inconsistent with eldership.

He must not be greedy of filthy lucre. The true bishop understands that money is to be used for the Lord and for the advancement of His interests. A grasping, greedy Christian is a paradox.

He must be patient. His Master was gentle, and the servant is not above his Master. Meekness and patience may not be virtues in the secular world, but they still are in the Kingdom of God.

He must not be a brawler, or contentious. Some are ready to fight at the drop of a hat, and to argue over matters of little consequence. Not so a bishop.

Then, again, he must not be covetous. To covet is to want something which God never intended one to have. Covetousness is idolatry, because it puts one's will above the will of God.

The elder must rule his own house well, having his children in subjection with all gravity—children who believe, and who are not accused of riot or unruly. The necessity for this requirement is obvious. "For if a man know not how to rule his own house, how shall he take care of the church of God?" (1 Timothy 3:5).

He must not be a novice. This is implied in the name "elder." Spiritual maturity is necessary. A man may be old in years, and yet not be qualified for spiritual oversight because of lack of experience as a Christian. The danger is that a novice becomes lifted up with pride, and falls into the condemnation of the devil.

He must have a good report of them that are without. The world should know that he is a man of Christian character and integrity.

He must not be self-willed, not soon angry, a lover of that which is good. He must be just and holy. Finally, he must hold fast the faithful word; that is, he must be a defender of the faith.

To summarize the qualifications of an elder, we might say that he must be able to control himself, he must be able to control his own home, and he must be a contender for the truth of God.

Now it should be noted that the Bible does not say the bishop must be an ordained clergyman. It does not say he must have a college degree. It does not say he must be a successful businessman. It is not of importance whether he is prominent in the community. Nothing is said about his personal appearance or the size of his bank balance. He might be a hunch-backed, ungainly, poor, old street-sweeper, and still be an elder in the church of God. Let us ponder this seriously. Doubtless one of the greatest blights on the church today is the recognition of men as elders who do not have the spiritual qualifications. Because a man has been successful in business, he is catapulted into a place of leadership in the church, even though he may have little or no spirituality. The result is an abundance of whatever money will buy and an absence of spiritual power.

THE DUTIES OF A BISHOP

What are the duties of elders? First of all they are to feed the flock of God (1 Peter 5:2; Acts 20:28). They do this by ministering the Word of God. It does not necessarily imply public ministry, but may be by visitation from house to house.

Secondly, they are to do the work of overseers. "Taking the oversight thereof," Peter writes. What does this mean? The rest of the passage explains what it does not mean, and what it does mean. It does not mean serving by constraint. This must be a willing service. It does not mean working for monetary gain. Not for filthy lucre, but of a ready mind. It does not mean lording it over God's heritage. The elder is not a dictator, not a taskmaster, not a boss. But it does mean being an example to the flock. The elder must remember that the Good Shepherd does not drive His sheep—He leads them. Every under-shepherd should do the same. From the human standpoint, it would be much easier to have centralized human authority in the church, so that orders could be issued from headquarters, and obedience would be mandatory.

But that is not God's way. The elders oversee the church by being examples to the flock.

In a very real way, the elders set the tone in a church. Where there are elders who are godly men, who put the Lord first in their lives, who radiate the grace of the Lord Jesus, one can expect to find a healthy, spiritual church; on the other hand, where the elders are engrossed in the affairs of the world, occupied with outside interests, too busy to read the Word or to pray, one can expect to find a coldness and deadness among the flock.

Again, the elders are told to support the weak. "I have showed you all things, how that so labouring ye ought to support the weak and to remember the words of the Lord Jesus, how He said, It is more blessed to give than to receive" (Acts 20:35). The context implies that they should be ready to help those who are in need by giving to them. That is an interesting thing. Instead of making a living off the flock, they should share their living with the flock.

Finally, the elders should reprove, rebuke and exhort (2 Timothy 4:2; Titus 1:13; 2:15). Whatever is contrary to the faith must be rebuked with all authority. Those who will not endure sound doctrine should be reproved and exhorted. The elder must earnestly contend for the faith.

What attitude should the church take toward elders? It is clear from 1 Timothy 5:17, 18 that some elders are cared for in a financial way by the church. "Let the elders that rule well be counted worthy of double honour, especially they who labour in the word and doctrine. For the Scripture saith, Thou shalt not muzzle the ox that treadeth out the corn. And, the labourer is worthy of his reward."

It is equally clear that others worked for their own support. Paul himself is an outstanding instance of this (1 Corinthians 4:12).

In addition, an elder is not to be rebuked, but entreated as a father (1 Timothy 5:1). Christians should not receive an accusation against an elder except before two or three witnesses (1 Timothy 5:19).

And then, the bishops should be remembered, recognized and obeyed. "Esteem them very highly in love for their work's sake" (1 Thessalonians 5:13). "Remember them which have the rule over you, who have spoken unto you the word of God: whose faith follow, considering the end of their conversation. Jesus Christ the same yesterday, and today, and for ever" (Hebrews 13:7, 8).

Finally, we note the rewards of the bishops. "When the chief Shepherd shall appear, ye shall receive a crown of glory that fadeth not away" (1 Peter 5:4).

When you are ready, complete Exam 5 by answering questions 11-19 on pages 99-102. (You should have already answered questions 1-10 as part of your study of lesson 9.)

CHRIST LOVED THE CHURCH

Exam

Name_____ Grade_____
(print plainly)

Address _____

City_____ State _____ Zip Code _____ Class Number _____

Instructor _____

LESSON 9

In the blank space in the right-hand margin write the letter of the correct answer. (45 points)

1. The Lord's supper was inaugurated
   a. by the Lord after He had celebrated the last Passover
   b. by the Lord in the upper room when He appeared to the disciples after His resurrection
   c. at a place called Emmaus where He was made known to two of His own "in the breaking of the bread"
   d. by the apostles on the Day of Pentecost _____

2. The Lord's supper is primarily a feast of
   a. repentance
   b. recognition
   c. remembrance
   d. restoration _____

3. Prominent in the celebration of the Lord's supper is
   a. the concept of transubstantiation
   b. the truth of the Lord's promised return
   c. the challenge to evangelize the lost
   d. the opportunity to pray for our own wants and needs _____

4. According to the New Testament the Lord's supper
   a. must be celebrated weekly
   b. was probably celebrated every week in the early church
   c. ought to be celebrated only at considerable intervals of time lest it become a mere habit
   d. was usually celebrated on the Sabbath day by the early church _____

5. The Lord's supper
   a. is for all who wish to participate
   b. is only for those ordained and in holy orders
   c. is for all believers without exception
   d. is for believers in fellowship with the Lord   _____

6. The Christian church was born in the wake of
   a. a gospel meeting
   b. a prayer meeting
   c. a testimony meeting
   d. a worship meeting   _____

7. The Lord has promised to be present when His people gather in His Name and to answer united prayer. This pledge is found in
   a. Matthew 18:19, 20
   b. John 15:7
   c. James 4:3
   d. 1 Timothy 2:2   _____

8. In public praying it is best to
   a. arrange for seasoned prayer warriors only to lead the saints to the throne of grace.
   b. give young converts a list of items for which to pray and to prescribe for them the proper form into which they should cast their prayers
   c. avoid being too specific
   d. keep prayers short   _____

9. List 5 things well worth praying for in the prayer meeting. *(5 points)*

   a. _____

   b. _____

   c. _____

   d. _____

   e. _____

10. Give three reasons, mentioned in the lesson, which would explain why some prayers are unanswered. *(5 points)*

a. _____

_____

b. _____

_____

c. _____

_____

WHAT DO YOU SAY?

Give one answer to prayer which has thrilled you.

_____

_____

_____

_____

LESSON 10

In the blank space in the right-hand margin write the letter of the correct answer. (28 points)

11. In the New Testament, a bishop is
   a. an appointed dignitary of the church
   b. an honorary officer of the church with the responsibility of overseeing the work of many local churches
   c. one of several mature Christians caring for the spiritual welfare of a given local church
   d. the chief elected officer in a local church   _____

12. In the New Testament the word "bishop" describes a person who is also described
   a. as an elder
   b. as an overseer
   c. as a presbyter
   d. in all the above ways _____

13. Scripturally, men are made bishops
   a. only by the Holy Spirit
   b. by popular vote of the local church
   c. by popular vote of a group of churches
   d. by appointment from a proper hierarchical headquarters _____

14. Paul's practice of appointing bishops
   a. is warrant enough for the church to continue with this practice
   b. is exceptional and was done because of the absence of Divinely written instructions at the time
   c. shows that bishops ought to be appointed as soon as a local church is established and without any waste of time or delay
   d. is clearly indicated in Acts 20:28 _____

15. According to Peter a bishop
   a. ought to be paid for his work
   b. should take the position against his will if pressured to do so
   c. has the right to give orders to other Christians and expect them to be implicitly obeyed
   d. must be able to lead _____

16. An elder in the assembly is found to be at fault. The correct thing to do is
   a. gossip about him
   b. rebuke him before the whole assembly
   c. plead with him to acknowledge his wrong
   d. to ignore the fault _____

17. Assuming no other qualification, which of the following would most likely be a scriptural elder? Each of the men described is a believer and in the fellowship of the local church.
   a. Henry Horder who is a prominent banker in such demand as a speaker at civic functions he rarely makes it to the mid-week prayer meeting
   b. Wally Wiseman, a professor in the local university, known to his students as "Powder-Keg" because of his notorious "short fuse" and hot temper
   c. Don Doughman, a wealthy and famous philanthropist, recently saved and showing great zeal
   d. Peter Potter who seems to have all the spiritual qualifications but who is sickly, shabby in appearance and a social nobody _____

18. Give a reason why you either rejected or else accepted in your own mind each of the following as an elder. (See question 17.) Give a Biblical reason for your position in each case. *(12 points)*

   a. Henry Horder: _____

   _____

   _____

   _____

   b. Wally Wiseman: _____

   _____

   _____

   _____

   c. Don Doughman: _____

   _____

   _____

   _____

   d. Peter Potter: _____

   _____

   _____

   _____

19. Turn in your Bible to Titus 1:6-9 and to 1 Timothy 3:1-7. Document each of the following statements concerning the qualifications of a bishop with the proper reference selected from the list given below. Simply write the correct identifying number (1, 2, etc.) on the appropriate line. *(10 points)*

(1)	1 Timothy 3:2		(6)	1 Timothy 3:4, 5
(2)	1 Timothy 3:2; Titus 1:6		(7)	1 Timothy 3:2; Titus 1:8
(3)	1 Timothy 3:3; Titus 1:7		(8)	1 Timothy 3:7
(4)	1 Timothy 3:3		(9)	1 Timothy 3:2; Titus 1:6, 7
(5)	Titus 1:9		(10)	1 Timothy 3:6

Qualifications   **Scripture choice**

a. The bishop must be blameless   _____

b. He must be hospitable   _____

c. He must be able to teach the Word   _____

d. He must not be materialistic   _____

e. His family must be well controlled   _____

f. He must be spiritually mature   _____

g. He must be known by the unsaved as a man of
Christian character and integrity   _____

h. He must be able to defend the faith   _____

i. He must be patient   _____

j. He must be a married man   _____

WHAT DO YOU SAY?

Describe the man in your local church who best fits the New Testament description of an elder—*NO NAMES PLEASE*—just a description of this person's qualifications.

_____

_____

_____

_____

_____

_____

_____

Those Who Serve

THE DEACONS

In our study of bishops, we learned that their function is the spiritual care and oversight of the house of God. We noted that bishops are also called elders, and that there are several bishops in one church, rather than one bishop over several churches.

We next come to the study of deacons, who they are and what their functions are.

1. What Are Deacons?

The word "deacon" simply means a servant—a man who pursues some ministry or service. Frequently in the New Testament it is used in this very general sense. For instance, a duly appointed civil official who rules in public affairs is called a deacon of God (Romans 13:4). Phebe is spoken of as a deaconess of the church of Cenchrea (Romans 16:1). Christ Himself is described as a deacon of the circumcision for the truth of God (Romans 15:8). The name has come to be applied to the seven men who were chosen in Acts 6:1-7, to take care of the disbursing of funds. Actually the word "deacon" is not found in that passage, and the word cannot be restricted to such duties. It applies to any form of service not otherwise designated.

2. Their Qualifications

Although the exact duties of deacons are nowhere specified, yet their qualifications are given with great explicitness in 1 Timothy 3. Beginning with verse 8, we read: "Likewise must the deacons be grave, not doubletongued, not given to much wine, not greedy of filthy lucre; Holding the mystery of the faith in a pure conscience. And let these also first be proved; then let them use the office of a deacon, being found blameless. Even so must their wives be grave, not slanderers, sober, faithful in all things. Let the deacons be the husbands of one wife, ruling their children and their own houses well. For they that have used the office of a deacon well, purchase to themselves a good degree, and great boldness in the faith which is in Christ Jesus."

The first requirement is gravity. A man who is lightheaded and frivolous will not be likely to gain the confidence of those whom he serves.

Then the deacon must not be doubletongued. That is, he must be consistent. He must not give one account to certain individuals and a different version to others. Honesty and straightforwardness are mandatory. Especially if his service involves handling funds, he should use such methods as will avoid the slightest possibility of suspicion or distrust.

He must not be given to much wine. No one can place confidence in an intemperate person. Experience teaches that intemperance and excess are the enemies of accuracy and dependability. They ruin a man's testimony for God and unfit him for divine service.

Also, he must not be greedy of filthy lucre. (Many of these requirements are identical with those of a bishop.) An avaricious spirit is a snare. If a man's heart is set on accumulating wealth, he can become so obsessed with this passion that every other activity in his life is made subservient to it. The Kingdom of God and His righteousness no longer hold first place in his life, and work for God is shoddy and unacceptable.

The deacon must hold the mystery of the faith in a pure

conscience. This is important. It is not enough for him to know the truth. He must practice the truth with a conscience void of offense toward God. Hymenaeus and Alexander both knew the Word of God, but they trifled with sin—that is, with evil doctrine (2 Timothy 2:17). They drowned out the voice of conscience and made shipwreck of the faith (1 Timothy 1:19, 20). There is no substitute for a tender conscience, one which is prompt to discern that which is displeasing to God, and to take sides with the Lord against it.

Next we read, "Let these also first be proved, then let them use the office of a deacon, being found blameless." This is a divine principle of considerable importance. "Let these also first be proved." In another passage, we read, "Lay hands suddenly on no man" (1 Timothy 5:22). It is a needed admonition for all of us. We are all prone to be impressed with a person the first time we meet him. We immediately want to advance him to a position of responsibility. Then after a time, we realize that it was a rash act. "All that glitters is not gold." We judged him on too short a notice.

The next qualification of deacons seems rather to deal with their wives. It reads, in the King James Version, "Even so must their wives be grave, not slanderers, sober, faithful in all things." However, we feel that J. N. Darby's translation is more to the point. It reads, "The women in like manner grave, not slanderers, sober, faithful in all things." The point is that the women referred to are not the wives of deacons, but rather those who are themselves deaconesses. Phebe was a deaconess (servant) (Romans 16: 1). It would be difficult to understand why there should be special requirements for wives of deacons, when no such requirements are found for wives of bishops. However, there is no difficulty if it be understood that the verse applies to women who are serving the local church.

As in the case of elders, we learn that a deacon must be the husband of one wife, ruling his own children and his own house well. We have already been reminded that if a man does not command respect and authority in his own home, it is hardly possible that he can do so in the church.

3. Their Rewards

Now the reward of the deacon is twofold. If a man serves well as a deacon, he purchases to himself a good degree. He gains for himself a good standing among his fellow saints and a good prospect of reward at the judgment seat of Christ. Secondly, he purchases to himself great boldness in the faith which is in Christ Jesus. True, the world looks upon such a goal as of little value. It is too mystical, intangible, vague. But to the child of God, it is more valuable than gold or precious stones.

With regard to the support of deacons, the same thing applies as in the case of bishops. There are some who engage in secular work, and who, therefore, provide for their own needs. Others devote themselves wholly to the work of the Lord and for all such the principle is: "They which preach the Gospel should live of the Gospel" (1 Corinthians 9:14), "Let him that is taught in the word communicate unto him that teacheth in all good things" (Galatians 6:6).

4. Conclusion

Now in closing our study on deacons, we should like to refer once again to Philippians 1:1. There we find three types of people mentioned as being in the church of God—saints, bishops and deacons. It is noteworthy that those are the only classes named. Saints first, then bishops, then deacons. The absence of another class known as the clergy is noteworthy, as has been pointed out by Barnes in his *Commentary on the New Testament:* "There are not 'three orders' of clergy in the New Testament. The apostle Paul in this chapter (1 Timothy 3) expressly designates the characteristics of those who should have charge of the church, but mentions only two, 'bishops' and 'deacons.' The former are ministers of the word, having charge of the spiritual interests of the church; the others are deacons, of whom there is no evidence that they were appointed to preach—there is no 'third' order. There is no allusion to anyone who was to be 'superior' to the 'bishops' and 'deacons.'

As the apostle Paul was expressly giving instructions in regard to the organization of the church, such an omission is unaccountable if he supposed there was to be an order of 'prelates' in the church. Why is there no allusion to them? Why is there no mention of their qualifications? If Timothy was himself a prelate, was he to have nothing to do in transmitting the office to others? Were there no peculiar qualifications required in such an order of men which it would be proper to mention? Would it not be *respectful*, at least, in Paul to have made some allusion to such an office, if Timothy himself held it?"[1]

The answer is, of course, that if the organization of the New Testament church contained any other order than bishops and deacons, then Paul would have mentioned it. The vast ecclesiastical systems of our day have been added by men, with no warrant whatever from the Word of God.

THE CHURCH'S FINANCES

Throughout the New Testament, it is both stated and implied that the church receives its finances from those who are within. There is no hint of any unsaved persons outside the church contributing to its support. Christian giving is an act of worship and is thus limited to those who have been redeemed by the precious blood of Christ. Neither is there any hint of a local church being financed, subsidized, or supported by any other church, group of churches, or council. Every local church should be self-supporting. The major teachings of the New Testament with regard to this important subject of the church's finances may readily be outlined.

1. Who Owns What?

All that a Christian has belongs to God. The believer is to act as a steward, using all he has in the best possible way for his Master's

---

[1] (London: Blackie & Son), Vol. VIII, p. 155.

glory. (See Luke 16:1-12.) F. B. Meyer stated the truth as follows: "We are meant to be stewards; not storing up our Lord's money for ourselves, but administering for Him all that we do not need for the maintenance of ourselves and our dear ones, in the position of life in which God has placed us. And our only worldly aim should be to lay out our Lord's money to the very best advantage; so that we may render Him an account with joy, when He comes to reckon with us."[1]

2. When and Where to Give

The Christian is instructed to give to the work of the Lord. When is he to give? "Upon the first day of the week, let every one of you lay by him in store" (1 Corinthians 16:2). How much is he to give? He is to give "as God has prospered him" (1 Corinthians 16: 2) and as Christ gave. He was rich, but became poor that we might be rich (2 Corinthians 8:9). He is our example. We should give out of our want, not out of our abundance (Mark 12:44). In short, the Christian should give liberally. The tithe (one tenth) was the minimum given by an Israelite. He brought tithes *and offerings*. No Christian should be content to give, under grace, what was the minimum requirement under law.

3. How to Give

In what spirit is he to give? He should first give himself to the Lord (2 Corinthians 8:5), thus acknowledging that all belongs to Him. Giving must be done in love (1 Corinthians 13:3), else it is valueless. It should be done in secret (Matthew 6:1-4)—so secret that the left hand does not know what the right hand is doing, to use a figure of speech. It should be done cheerfully, not grudgingly (2 Corinthians 9:7). We find that the early Christians sold their possessions and shared their wealth with one another (Acts 2:44,

---

[1] Meyer, F. B., *Elijah: And the Secret of His Power* (London: Morgan and Scott, No date given), p. 52.

45; 4:31-37). This was an outward expression of their true spiritual fellowship. Such action is nowhere commanded in the New Testament. In fact, the instructions of Scripture concerning Christian giving presuppose private ownership of property. The action by the early church was purely voluntary. It is not to be confused with monasticism or with the "communism" of today.

4.   The Reward

What are the rewards for giving? When we are faithful in the unrighteous mammon (in the use of our money), God will commit true riches (spiritual treasures) to our trust (Luke 16:11). Fruit abounds to the account of the giver (Philippians 4:17). He will have treasures in Heaven (Matthew 6:19-21), because his gifts are "an odour of a sweet smell, a sacrifice acceptable, well-pleasing to God" (Philippians 4:18).

5.   The Assembly Treasurer

Those who handle the funds of the church should use business methods that are above reproach. "Provide for honest things, not only in the sight of the Lord, but also in the sight of men" (2 Corinthians 8:21). At least two men should be appointed to take charge of the offering. In Acts 6:1-6 we read that seven men were appointed to handle the distribution of funds to widows in the assembly. The Epistles contain no definite instructions as to exactly how many men should handle the money, but it is clear from 1 Corinthians 16:3, 4 and 2 Corinthians 8:18, 19 that it was customary to entrust this responsibility to more than one. In the former passage, Paul states that he would send *those* whom the Corinthians approved with the offering to Jerusalem, and, if necessary, he would go, too. Note the plurals—"them" (verse 3); "they" (verse 4). In the latter reference, Paul explains that another brother was chosen to travel with him in distributing the gift from the church.

6. The Giving of the Local Church

The New Testament reveals three principal purposes for which the funds of the church are expended. These are for widows in the assembly, for poor saints and for those who devote their time to preaching and teaching the Word.

For widows in the assembly (Acts 6:1-6). In order to qualify as a "widow indeed" (1 Timothy 5:3-16), a woman had to meet the following requirements. (1) She had to be desolate; that is, without any relatives who could support her, and utterly cast upon the Lord for her needs (vv. 4, 5, 16). (2) She had to be at least sixty years old. (3) She had to be known for her good works, her noble motherhood, her hospitality, and her charity (see v. 10).

For the poor saints. God has exhorted us many times in His Word to remember the poor (e.g., Galatians 2:10; Romans 12:13); and the prosperity of His people in the Old Testament is closely linked with their treatment of their needy brethren (Deuteronomy 14:29). Around A.D. 45, many of the Christians in Judea were stricken with poverty. This was probably due to severe persecution and widespread famine. The saints in Antioch sent relief to the Judean brethren by the hands of Barnabas and Saul (Acts 11:27-30). The assembly at Corinth was urged to do the same thing (1 Corinthians 16:1-3; 2 Corinthians 8 and 9). We are likewise responsible to care for those in need. The Lord Jesus said, "Ye have the poor with you always" (Mark 14:7). It is good for an assembly to have poor members whom it can care for with a godly exercise. Barnes points out that a great way to unite Christians and to prevent alienation and jealousy and strife is to have a common object of charity, in which all are interested and to which all may contribute. The assembly is not, however, responsible for those who are poor because they do not want to work. In such cases the divine decree is that, if any man will not work, neither shall he eat (2 Thessalonians 3:10).

For those who devote their time to the work of the Lord. It is a divine principle that those who preach the Gospel or teach the Word are entitled to the support of the saints. "Let him who is receiving instruction in the Word give ungrudgingly a share of his worldly goods to him who instructs him" (Galatians 6:6, Way's Translation). (See also 1 Corinthians 9:4-13; 1 Timothy 5:17, 18.)

Oftentimes, however, the Apostle Paul labored with his hands, rather than accept fellowship from assemblies (Acts 18:3). His reasons for this were simple. He wanted to serve as an example to the Ephesians, that they, too, might support the weak and know the blessedness of giving (Acts 20:33-35). He also wished to prevent his critics in Corinth from charging him with mercenary motives (2 Corinthians 11:7-12). In addition he desired to prevent the Thessalonian believers from being burdened with his support (1 Thessalonians 2:9; 2 Thessalonians 3:7-9). The saints there were poor and were being persecuted.

The assembly at Philippi was commended for ministering to Paul (Philippians 4:10-19). Note that Paul did not desire the fellowship because of his need, but because he wanted fruit to abound to their account.

Note, also, that although the Apostle never publicized his personal needs, he did not hesitate to make known the needs of other saints (2 Corinthians 8 and 9). There is, thus, a difference between information and solicitation. As Dr. Chafer has pointed out—"All will agree that information is required, else no intelligent giving is possible; but the real problem centers around the question of solicitation."

7. Conclusion

The reader of the New Testament will notice how delightfully simple is the financing of the church. There are no burdensome, legalistic rules, neither is there an elaborate, complex financial organization. If the simple precepts of the Scripture were followed, two important results would ensue. The needs of the church would be liberally supplied without solicitations. The church would not have to be reproached by the world as a money-making institution.

When you have mastered this lesson, take the first part of Exam 6 (covering lesson 11, questions 1-10 on pages **123-125** (right after lesson 12).

Taking Our Place

THE MINISTRY OF WOMEN

Definite instructions are given in the New Testament concerning the position and service of women in the church. We shall now summarize these instructions.

1. The Primary Matter

With regard to such matters as salvation or acceptance before God, woman is on an equality with man. "There is neither male nor female: for ye are all one in Christ Jesus" (Galatians 3:28). This does not mean, however, that differences of sex are abolished in the church. When dealing with matters of everyday life, the Scriptures distinguish between male and female. For instance, in Ephesians 5 we have the admonitions: "Wives, submit yourselves unto your own husbands" (v. 22); "Husbands, love your wives" (v. 25). Therefore, we may say that as far as her standing before God is concerned, woman is treated exactly the same as man; but that as far as her position in the church is concerned, a distinction is made. The distinction, in brief, is that woman should be in subjection to the man (1 Corinthians 11:3).

2. Accentuating the Negative

Specifically, the following injunctions are laid down in the Word in order to define the various ways in which the subjection of the woman is to be manifested. She must remain silent in the church (1 Corinthians 14:34, 35). What is meant by "remaining silent" is further explained. She is not permitted to teach (1 Timothy 2:12). She should not ask questions publicly (1 Corinthians 14:35). She should learn in silence with all subjection (1 Timothy 2:11). She must not usurp authority over the man (1 Timothy 2:12). She must not pray or prophesy with her head uncovered (1 Corinthians 11:5). That this does not permit women praying publicly in the church, however, is strongly implied in 1 Timothy 2:8, "I will therefore that *men* pray every where." Here the word used for "men" means "males" in contrast to "females." The Greek word employed here excludes women.

If these instructions are forced on women in a harsh, legalistic spirit, the result is usually twofold. God is not pleased with an enforced obedience which does not spring from the heart (Psalm 51:17). The women themselves are apt to become bitter and resentful. If, on the other hand, the reasons for such instructions are clearly understood, and there follows the obedience of a loving, submissive heart, then this is of great price in the sight of the Lord (1 Samuel 15:22).

3.   Reasons Why

God has graciously condescended to state certain underlying principles in His Word in order to explain why Christian women should be in subjection to the men.

First of all, in the order of creation, man had priority over the woman. "Adam was first formed, then Eve" (1 Timothy 2:13). "The man is not of the woman; but the woman of the man" (1 Corinthians 11:8). The argument here is that the order instituted by God in creation is the order which He intends to be maintained in the church; namely, the head of the woman is the man (1 Corinthians 11:3).

Secondly, the purpose of creation indicates the headship of the man over the woman. "Neither was the man created for the woman; but the woman for the man" (1 Corinthians 11:9).

Thirdly, sin entered into the world when Eve usurped authority over her husband, Adam. "Adam was not deceived, but the woman being deceived was in the transgression" (1 Timothy 2:14). The Lord does not wish His new creation to be marred through this type of insubjection, and so He has instructed the women to be under obedience.

In the fourth place, Paul appeals to the consistent testimony of the Old Testament Scriptures to show that women should be under obedience (1 Corinthians 14:34). "They are commanded to be under obedience, as also saith the law." While no particular commandment states this clearly, yet it is the tenor of the Old Testament.

4. The Covered Head

With regard to the instruction that women should be covered (or veiled) when praying or prophesying, two additional reasons are presented. Angels are looking on. "For this cause ought the woman to have a sign of authority on her head, because of the angels" (1 Corinthians 11:10, R.V.). This verse seems to picture the angelic hosts observing God's order on the earth, and it states that women should wear a covering on their head as a sign or badge of the authority of the man. Thus, the angels see that the transgression of Eve in the first creation is not perpetuated in the new creation.

The lesson is taught by nature itself. "Doth not even nature itself teach you . . ." (1 Corinthians 11:14). In the original creation, God gave women a distinctive covering—that of long hair. Paul argues from this that a divine principle is illustrated thereby; namely, that woman should wear a veil or covering over her head when praying or prophesying.

5. Accentuating the Positive

The fact that woman is in subjection to the man might seem to indicate to some that she has no place or ministry in God's

115

economy. However, the Scriptures contradict this by showing that woman's ministry, though not a public one, is nonetheless real and important. Her position is saved by childbearing (1 Timothy 2: 15). This difficult verse might mean that a godly mother, though restrained from ministering publicly, is not thereby relegated to a place of uselessness. Her position is to rear her family in the fear and admonition of the Lord. If she and her husband continue in the faith, she may one day have sons to preach and teach the Word. Thus the expression, "she shall be saved," might refer, not to the soul's salvation, or even to being saved from physical death in the act of childbearing, but rather to the salvation of woman's place and privilege. She will not become a nonentity, but will have this glorious ministry of rearing children to live for God's glory.

Other examples of women's ministry are found in the New Testament, such as ministering of their substance (Luke 8:3), showing hospitality (Romans 16:1), and teaching the younger women (Titus 2:4).

6. Some Common Objections

Numerous objections and questions arise in connection with the subject of women's ministry. Does not Paul's teaching on this subject, it is argued, represent the views of an unmarried man with a prejudice against women? No! They are teachings of the Holy Spirit of God, or, as Paul wrote in 1 Corinthians 14:37, "the commandments of the Lord."

Then it is asked if Paul was merely teaching what was a local custom in his day without any idea that this state of things should be applicable to us today. The answer is that his first epistle to the Corinthians was written not only to the church of God in Corinth, but to "all that in every place call upon the name of Jesus Christ our Lord" (1 Corinthians 1:2). Therefore the instructions are of universal application.

But, we are asked, does not Paul indicate in 1 Corinthians 11:16 that the things that he had been teaching were not binding, and that such customs were not practiced among the churches of

God? ("But if any man seem to be contentious, we have no such custom, neither the churches of God.") Such an interpretation undermines the inspiration and authority of the Bible. What the verse really says is that contention about these commandments of the Lord was not a custom in the churches. The churches accepted them and obeyed them, without arguing or explaining them away.

Since woman's hair is given to her for a covering, it is argued, is not that the only covering that is required? There are two coverings in 1 Corinthians 11. A woman's hair is mentioned as a covering in verse 15, but a veil is necessarily in view in verse 5. Otherwise verse 6 would be saying in effect, "For if a woman does not have her hair on, let her also be shorn, but if it be a shame for a woman to be shorn or shaven, let her put her hair on." Obviously such a meaning is impossible. It must mean that a covering, other than her hair, is necessary.

Does not the instruction for women to keep silence in the church (1 Corinthians 14:34), merely prohibit their chattering or gossiping while the service is in progress? No! The passage says, "It is not permitted unto them to speak." The word translated "speak" here never has the meaning of "chatter" or "babble" in the New Testament. The same word is used of God in verse 21, "With men of other tongues . . . will I speak."

Many additional questions arise, such as whether it is all right for women to give a testimony in public, to give an account of their missionary work, to sing a solo. Where individual cases are not specifically dealt with in the Bible, then the general principles of the Word must be allowed to decide. Thus, in any doubtful situation, we should ask: Does this constitute a usurping of authority over the man? Is woman taking a place of leadership? Is she teaching the Word? Since these things are prohibited, we should avoid anything that might constitute an infringement of the spirit of these teachings of the Word.

7.   God's Wisdom is Manifest

God's design in setting forth these instructions was His people's good as well as His own glory. Where His Word has been ignored or wilfully violated, strife and disorder have ensued. The positive evil of women usurping authority and teaching publicly is seen in the rise of many cults—notably Seventh Day Adventism, Theosophy, Christian Science—in which women had a prominent role.

On the other hand, nothing is more comely and pleasant than to see Christian women occupying their God-appointed place and exhibiting "the ornament of a meek and quiet spirit" (1 Peter 3:4).

LET US GO FORTH UNTO HIM!

In the previous pages, we have discussed the church, both from its universal aspect and its local aspect. We have sought to discover the principles of the church as taught in the New Testament, and to catch the simplicity, zeal, and spirituality of the assembly as it existed in the days of the apostles. Now the question remains, "What is the application of all this to believers in the twentieth century?"

1. The Church Today

In order to answer this question, we should first take a brief look at conditions in the professing church today. On every hand we find departure, failure, and ruin. We find vast ecclesiastical organizations combining material wealth and political influence but largely devoid of spiritual power. We find denominationalism and sectarianism claiming the loyalty and support of their adherents, yet presenting a faithless and perverted view of the church. We find the meetings of the church occupied with a lifeless liturgy and a soul-deadening ritualism, offering the people shadows instead of Christ. We find a clerical system which has reduced the average layman to a dumb priest if not a mere coin-dispensing machine. We find churches with membership rolls including both saved and unsaved, both true believers and those with no vital union with the living Savior. Finally, we find churches that have been corrupted with the leaven of modernism, that have substituted a social gospel for the message of redeeming grace.

2. The Need for Separation

If it be asked what a Christian should do who finds himself in such a situation, there can only be one answer. Separate from it! Go forth unto Him without the camp! The Word of God is mercilessly uncompromising in its insistence that believers should withdraw themselves from every form of evil—whether ecclesiastical, doctrinal, or moral. "Be ye not unequally yoked together with unbelievers: for what fellowship hath righteousness with unrighteousness? And what communion hath light with darkness? And what concord hath Christ with Belial? Or what part hath he that believeth with an infidel? And what agreement hath the temple of God with idols? For ye are the temple of the living God; as God hath said, I will dwell in them, and walk in them; and I will be their God, and they shall be my people. Wherefore come out from among them, and be ye separate, saith the Lord, and touch not the unclean thing; and I will receive you, and will be a Father unto you, and ye shall be my sons and daughters, saith the Lord Almighty" (2 Corinthians 6:14-18).

It is vain to argue that a Christian should remain within a corrupt church in order to be a voice for God in it. "There is not a single hero or saint, whose name sparkles on the inspired pages, who moved his times from within: all, without exception, have raised the cry, 'Let us go forth without the camp;' . . . The man who goes into the world to level it up will soon find himself levelled down. . . . The safest and strongest position is outside the camp. Archimedes said he could move the world, if only he had a point of rest given him outside it. Thus, too, can a handful of God's servants influence their times, if only they resemble Elijah, whose life was spent altogether outside the pale of the court and the world of his time."[1]

"To all who argue for a continuance in a church position which they know to be wrong, Samuel furnishes a pointed and

---

[1] Meyer, F. B., *Elijah: And the Secret of His Power* (London: Morgan & Scott, No date given), pp. 65, 66.

powerful reply—'To obey is better than sacrifice, and to hearken than the fat of rams.' "[1]

3.   What Next?

But the question still remains, "What should a person do after he has obeyed the scriptural injunction to 'come out'?" In answer to this, we would suggest the following scriptural plan.

Gather together in Christian simplicity with a group of like-minded believers.

Gather to Christ alone; make Him the sole attraction. Though such a policy will not result in large crowds, it will at least provide a nucleus of faithful believers who will not be easily moved by trials or discouragements.

As far as a meeting place is concerned, a home is entirely satisfactory, and has a great deal of scriptural precedent (Romans 16:5; 1 Corinthians 16:19; Colossians 4:15; Philemon 2). Those who require a splendid edifice with religious hardware have never really discovered the all-sufficiency of the Lord Jesus as the Person to whom His people gather.

Adopt no name or policy that would exclude any true believer from the fellowship.

Adopt no denominational affiliation, and stedfastly refuse any outside control or interference that would infringe on the sovereignty of the local church.

Resist the constant tendency to allow the ministry to drift into the hands of one man. Rather allow the Holy Spirit to use the various gifts which Christ has given to the church, and provide for the active manifestation of the priesthood of all believers.

Gather together regularly for prayer, study of the Word, breaking of bread, and fellowship. Then engage in an active gospel effort, both individually and collectively.

In short, seek to meet as a New Testament church in the

---

[1] Mackintosh, C. H., *Notes on Genesis* (New York: Loizeaux Bros., 1951), p. 155.

trucst sense of the word by giving a faithful representation of the body of Christ and by obeying the commandments of the Lord.

4. Those Who Have Come Out

Interestingly enough, this is being done by Christians all over the world today. With no guide-book but the Bible, they have found these principles to be divine, and have followed them in spite of reproach and slander. They own no head but Christ, no fellowship but His Body, no headquarters but His throne. They seek in true humility to witness to the unity of the body of Christ. In their fellowship, they seek to provide a sanctuary for true believers who are oppressed by modernism and related evils. There is no directory on earth that lists these churches, nothing of an earthly nature to bind them together. Their only unity is that which is formed and maintained by the Holy Spirit, and they are content that it should be so.

There is no reason why hundreds of similar fellowships should not be formed by the Great Head of the church through the sacrificial and prayerful exercise of His people. Where Christians have caught the vision, and are willing to suffer for it, the Lord will reward their exercise and endeavors, and fulfill their longings for His glory.

Is it possible that on the very eve of the Lord's return, we are about to see a great revolt led by the Holy Spirit against apostate Christendom, and a fresh, new movement of His grace, forming small, independent fellowships of Bible-loving Christians?

May He who loved the church, and gave Himself for it, bring it to pass, for His own glory!

When you are ready, complete Exam 6 by answering questions 11-19 on pages 125-128. (You should have already answered questions 1-10 as part of your study of lesson 11.)

CHRIST LOVED THE CHURCH

Name_____
(print plainly)

Exam
Grade_____

Address _____

| | | Zip | Class |
City_____ State _____ Code _____ Number _____

Instructor _____

LESSON 11

In the blank space in the right-hand margin write the letter of the correct answer.
(45 points)

1. In the New Testament the word "deacon"
   a. is synonymous with the word "elder"
   b. refers to those who serve on a church board and to whom the local pastor is responsible
   c. is first used to describe the seven men set apart by the Jerusalem church to handle its mundane affairs
   d. simply means a servant and it applies to those who serve   _____

2. Which of the following is **NOT** given specifically in the New Testament as a qualification of a deacon? He must be
   a. temperate
   b. the father of many children
   c. honest
   d. grave   _____

3. In New Testament times
   a. a woman could be a deacon
   b. no woman could serve as a deacon
   c. only those women who were wives of deacons could hold a like position
   d. all women were deacons   _____

123

4. In the New Testament only three classes are envisioned in the church. These are
a. monks, priests and nuns
b. saints, bishops and deacons
c. pastors, deacons and laity
d. popes, cardinals and bishops

_____

5. The finances of the church
a. must come from Christians only
b. can be raised in any manner so long as no dishonest practices are employed
c. may be solicited from unsaved people only when the believers are unable to handle the burden alone
d. can be raised scripturally by soliciting the support of large secular foundations

_____

6. The New Testament teaches that Christians should give
a. a tithe of their income only
b. proportionately, as God has prospered
c. only when they are in a lucrative financial condition
d. only in response to high-pressure appeals

_____

7. What kind of a giver does the New Testament specifically state that _"God loves"_
a. a generous giver
b. a regular giver
c. a cheerful giver
d. a secret giver

_____

8. In disbursing its funds, the local church should
a. support all widows in its fellowship
b. remember the poor
c. give to those who are able but, for one reason or another, are unwilling to work
d. make sure the pastor has an adequate salary

_____

9. The apostle Paul
a. never accepted financial support for himself
b. refused to do secular work on the grounds that those engaged in spiritual work should be fully supported at all times by those with secular employment
c. never publicized financial needs
d. praised the Philippians for ministering to him financially

_____

10. State two important results which would ensue if scriptural precepts were followed in the matter of the church's finances. *(5 points)*

a. _____

_____

b. _____

_____

WHAT DO YOU SAY?

Share one incident in which the Lord specifically led you in the matter of giving to His work.

_____

_____

_____

_____

LESSON 12

In the blank space in the right-hand margin write the letter of the correct answer. (40 points)

11. So far as her standing before God is concerned, woman
   a. is treated quite differently from man
   b. is treated exactly the same as man
   c. is given a position inferior to that of man
   d. is given a position superior to that of man   _____

12. When the Scripture enjoins a woman to "remain silent" it
    a. discriminates against women
    b. forbids her even the right to pray when only other women are present
    c. refers only to single women
    d. further elaborates so that the extent of the restriction can be measured

13. The reason why Paul enjoins silence on a woman in the church is that
    a. woman had her chance at headship in the original ordering of things at the creation
    b. the Old Testament placed the woman in authority over the man but the New Testament reverses this order
    c. the woman was deceived, NOT the man, at the original temptation
    d. man is of the woman, not woman of the man

14. The fact that angels are observing God's order on the earth is advanced by Paul as one reason why the woman should
    a. remain silent in the church
    b. be keepers at home
    c. have large families
    d. cover their heads when praying or prophesying

15. The expression "she shall be saved in child-bearing" refers
    a. to the salvation of the soul
    b. to a woman's emancipation in the rearing of children to live for God's glory
    c. to the coming of the Lord Jesus as "the seed of the woman" to be the world's Savior
    d. to all the above

16. To the argument "a woman's hair is her covering"
    a. it must be conceded that this adequately explains 1 Corinthians 11:5, 15
    b. it can be properly replied that two coverings are in view in 1 Corinthians 11
    c. it is best to reply that such a statement is contentious
    d. it should be pointed out that so is the man's

17. When Paul said of women that "it is not permitted unto them to speak" (1 Corinthians 14:34)
    a. he used a word usually rendered "chatter" elsewhere in the New Testament
    b. he was merely stating a personal preference, not a divine command
    c. he was displaying personal prejudice
    d. he was giving expression to a divine injunction _____

18. When faced with a church order which is definitely contrary to God's Word, the thing to do is
    a. stay and try to change things
    b. keep quiet about it so as not to disturb the peace but quietly to live for God despite the condition
    c. leave only if the disorder is moral
    d. leave so that God can use you elsewhere _____

19. What should a person do after he has obeyed the Scriptural injunction to "come out" from among them and be separate? *(10 points)*

    a. _____

    _____

    b. _____

    _____

    c. _____

    _____

    d. _____

    _____

    e. _____

    _____

WHAT DO YOU SAY?

How has this course helped you most?

_____

_____

_____

_____

_____